READING INTO
SCIENCE
BIOLOGY

Peter Ellis

D0320221

Published in 2003 by:
Nelson Thornes Ltd
Delta Place
27 Bath Road
CHELTENHAM
GL53 7TH
United Kingdom

03 04 05 06 / 10 9 8 7 6 5 4 3 2 1

A catalogue record for this book is available from the British Library

ISBN 0 7487 6799 1

Illustrations by Ian Foulis, Francis Bacon and Mike Bastin
Design and page make-up by Jordan Publishing Design

Printed and bound in Spain by Graficas

INTRODUCTION

The *Reading Into Science* series is for the Ideas and Evidence part of your GCSE. It covers a whole range of topics from historical figures to interviews with some real scientists who are making discoveries now. Some articles describe the work of scientists who had ideas that we do not agree with today. These articles show how our theories change as we collect new evidence. Other articles look at controversial topics, such as the use of pesticides and gene therapy. These articles will help you to make up your own mind!

Some articles are harder to read than others. Blue arrows show the more complicated ones. Red arrows show which ones are more straightforward.

There are questions at the end of each article. Use these to practise answering the sort of questions you will get in your final exam and to discuss issues raised with other students.

Finally there are web site addresses in case you want to follow up any of the ideas – or you can check out the *Reading Into Science* web site on **www.nelsonthornes.com/ris**. You will find the Ideas and Evidence requirements of your GCSE specification there and the statements covered by each article.

I hope you find these articles interesting and stimulating to read. I had a lot of fun preparing them. Let me know what you thought through the Nelson Thornes web site.

Best wishes

Peter Ellis

CONTENTS

MICROBES FIGHT BACK!

In 1928, Alexander Fleming found a mould on some bacteria test dishes. The mould had killed all the bacteria around it. He tested the mould but didn't develop a medicine. It wasn't until 1939 that Howard Florey and Ernst Chain started work to turn the mould into the first antibiotic drug. It was called penicillin. The new drug arrived just in time to help soldiers who had been wounded or infected by diseases in the Second World War.

« The penicillin men – Fleming, Florey and Chain »

Using antibiotics

Antibiotics kill bacteria. Since they were discovered they have been used in lots of different ways. Only about half of all the antibiotics that are manufactured are taken by humans to cure diseases. The rest are:

- given to farm animals in their food to help them grow bigger and stronger
- sprayed on fruit trees to kill bacteria before the fruit is picked
- put in cleaning fluids and hand lotions to kill bacteria found in the home.

What is resistance?

When bacteria meet an antibiotic, most of them die, but some survive. The survivors have a gene that protects them from the antibiotic. The survivors are resistant to the antibiotic. Now that all the other bacteria are dead the resistant bacteria have no competition for food. They divide over and over again. All the new bacteria are resistant.

Why are some bacteria resistant?

Bacteria grow and divide very quickly. This makes mutations more likely than in larger organisms. Mutations cause changes in the genes of a bacterium. Some of the mutated genes may make the bacterium resistant to antibiotics. Bacteria also swap genes with each other.

If one bacterium develops a resistant gene, then the bacteria around it can also quickly become resistant.

Why is resistance a problem?

We have been using antibiotics for over 60 years. In that time some disease bacteria have developed resistance to all the known antibiotics. When people become ill with these bacteria there is nothing doctors can do to help them. For example, the disease tuberculosis had almost disappeared from the UK. Now tuberculosis bacteria that are resistant to antibiotics are spreading and more people are becoming ill.

What have we done to help bacteria become resistant?

Every time we use an antibiotic there is a risk that some bacteria might survive. We may unknowingly help the resistance in many ways. For example:

- By not completing a course of treatment. You may have recovered from an illness but some bacteria may still be left. If you do not continue to take the antibiotic until the course is finished the bacteria that remain may develop resistance.
- By taking antibiotics when it is not necessary. Colds, flu and other common diseases are caused by viruses. Antibiotics have no effect on viruses. Taking the antibiotic kills harmless bacteria and removes competition for the resistant bacteria.

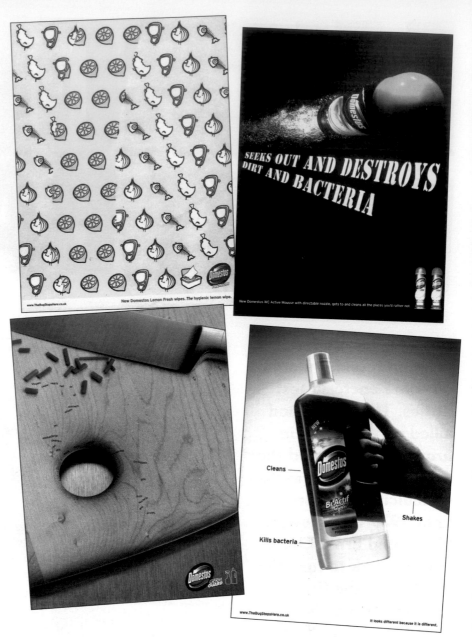

« **Many modern household cleaners contain substances that kill bacteria** »

- Using antibiotics in agriculture has the same effect. It allows resistant bacteria to multiply.
- Using antibiotic cleaning fluids and washing liquids also destroys harmless bacteria and gives resistant bacteria a chance to multiply.

What can we do to help?

- Always finish any tablets given to you by a doctor.

- Do not ask a doctor for antibiotics for illnesses where they won't work, such as colds and flu.
- Wash fruit and vegetables before eating them raw.
- Do not use household cleaners and washing liquids that contain antibiotics.
- Support campaigns to stop the use of antibiotics in agriculture.

KYLIE'S FLU

Kylie didn't feel well. Her head ached, her arms and legs ached. She struggled home from school and went to bed.

"You've got flu," said Kylie's mother. Kylie curled up under the bedclothes and tried to get comfortable but she still felt terrible.

Next morning, Kylie was worse. Her mother got worried and called the doctor. The doctor said "Kylie's got flu."

"She needs some tablets," Kylie's mother said.

"Antibiotics won't help her," the doctor replied. Kylie's mother cried and demanded that the doctor do something. The doctor did not have time to argue so he wrote a prescription for an antibiotic.

Kylie took the tablets. A few days later she felt better and got up. Next day she felt fit and well and went back to school.

« Does she need antibiotics? »

BEN'S CHICKEN SANDWICH

One evening Ben felt hungry. There wasn't much in the fridge because he hadn't bothered to go shopping. There was a piece of chicken left over from a meal last week and some stale bread. Ben ate it.

During the night Ben started feeling ill. His stomach hurt and he was sick. Ben called his housemate who called the doctor. The doctor arrived.

"You've got food poisoning," he said, "take these tablets."

Ben took the tablets and within a couple of days he felt a lot better. Although he still had some tablets left he felt fine so he didn't bother to take any more.

« Is that chicken fit to eat? »

FARMER PARKER'S PIGS

Farmer Parker was worried about his new litter of pigs. They weren't growing as quickly as they should. The vet came to the farm and gave farmer Parker an antibiotic to put in the pigs' food. Soon they were growing faster. Farmer Parker was pleased.

NATALIE'S GRANDMOTHER

"We must go and see Gran in hospital," said Natalie's mother. She sprayed a cleaner over the kitchen worktop and wiped it.

"What's wrong with Gran?" asked Natalie.

"She fell and broke her hip. She's old and frail and it happens very easily. I'm sure she will get better."

Natalie and her mother arrived at the hospital but found that they could not see Gran.

"We've had to move her to another ward," said the nurse. "She's caught an infection and the antibiotics do not seem to be working." Natalie's grandmother was kept separate from other patients. Only doctors and nurses wearing gloves and masks were allowed near her. Natalie waved through the window to her, but Gran didn't have the strength to wave back.

Days passed and the doctors tried lots of different medicines to cure Gran's illness, but none of them worked. She died.

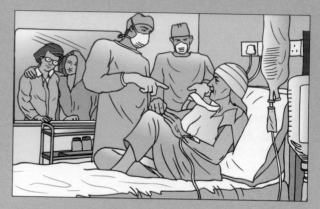

« A patient with a disease that is resistant to antibiotics must be kept isolated »

Read the case studies above. In each story something has been done that has helped bacteria to become resistant to antibiotics. For each story, write down what you think it is. ■

Questions

1 What happened to people who had diseases caused by bacteria before antibiotics were discovered?

2 Why is it pointless to take an antibiotic for a cold or flu?

Discussion

Some people have said, 'the discovery of antibiotics was the best thing to happen in medicine and the growth of resistant bacteria could be the biggest disaster.' Do you agree?

Extra activities

1 Look out for stories in newspapers or on TV news programmes about infections in hospitals.

Why do diseases spread quickly in hospitals?

What do the hospital authorities do when there is an infection in a ward?

2 Try this exercise to show how bacteria develop resistance.

Start with one bacterium. It divides into two new bacteria every half an hour.

Six hours pass. How many bacteria do you have?

An antibiotic kills all the bacteria except one. This bacterium is resistant. Another six hours pass. How many bacteria do you have?

3 Find out more about Fleming, Florey and Chain. They all won the Nobel Prize in 1945 for their work on penicillin.

WEBSITES

http://www.sciam.com/1998/0398issue/0398levy.html

GIVING BLOOD

The story of blood transfusions

The National Blood Transfusion Service urges us to 'Do something amazing today'. They want donors to give blood to save lives. Sharing blood has been something people have wanted to do for centuries, but it is only in the last 50 years that it has become common. Who carried out the first transfusion? Does everyone agree that it is a good idea? What problems were there and how were they solved? What is the future of blood transfusions?

« The National Blood Transfusion Service is always asking for new donors »

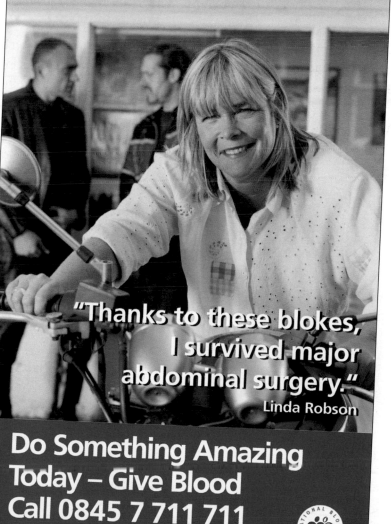

"Thanks to these blokes, I survived major abdominal surgery."
Linda Robson

Blood transfusion

It was a day in 1667 when Antoine Mauroy was brought to Jean Baptiste Denis' rooms in Paris. Mauroy was a 16-year-old boy who was kept under lock and key because of his mad, violent behaviour. His gaolers thought that Denis, the doctor to King Louis XIV, might be able to help him. Denis had been experimenting with passing blood from one animal to another and here was his chance to try it out on a living person.

Mauroy was strapped down on a bed. Using a silver tube, Denis extracted about a quarter of a litre of blood from a calf and injected it into Mauroy. The patient seemed to be unaffected and a few days later the operation was repeated. Mauroy's madness didn't disappear and six months later he was dead.

The people of Paris were appalled by Denis' experiment even though there was no proof that it had killed Mauroy. By 1670, a law was passed banning the giving of blood to humans. It seemed that the story of blood transfusion was over before it had really started.

Objections

Why did the passing of blood from one creature to another cause so much anger? The answer was religion. For Christians and believers of other religions, blood is special. Blood is the life-giving fluid. Who knows what might happen if the blood of one person was mixed with the blood of another. Would the blood donor also pass on parts of their personality, their faults and their sins?

The death of Mauroy and other subjects of experiments in blood transfusion also raised ethical questions. A doctor was trained to follow the Hippocratic oath – to do no harm. Transferring blood from one person to another obviously did cause harm.

Experiments go on

While blood transfusions were banned in France, elsewhere, bold experimenters continued to try it out. James Blundell carried out the first successful transfusion of blood from one person to another, in England, in 1818. His patient was a young woman who had lost a lot of blood after giving birth.

Unfortunately many experiments ended in the death of the patients.

Blundell decided to replace it by giving her some of her husband's blood. He injected about an eighth of a litre using a syringe. The woman survived. Between 1825 and 1830, Blundell carried out ten more transfusions, about half of which were successful.

Unfortunately many experiments ended in the death of the patients. It wasn't until late in the 19th century that someone realised what was happening. Often when blood from two people was mixed together it formed clumps, which blocked blood vessels.

Matching blood

The problem of blood matching was solved by Karl Landsteiner. Landsteiner was born in Vienna, Austria in 1868. He studied medicine and remained in Vienna until 1919. During this time Karl

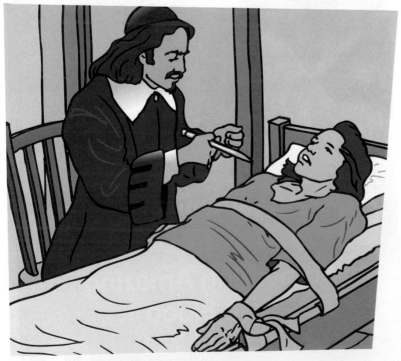

« Jean Baptiste Denis injects blood from a calf into Mauroy »

investigated the clumping of blood. He found that many people had one or two substances called antigens in their blood that caused the clumping. This gave rise to blood being divided into four groups – A, B, AB and O. If the blood of two people with different anitgens was mixed, the antigen from one made the other's blood cells clump together. Karl found that by carefully matching the blood types, blood from different people could be mixed without the clumping happening. Now it would be possible to give transfusions without any dangers to the patient receiving the blood. Karl moved to the Netherlands in 1919 and on to the USA in 1922. In 1930, he won the Nobel Prize for his work on blood types. Later the rhesus positive and rhesus negative blood types were discovered which meant that there were now eight different blood types.

There was still a major problem, however. Unless the blood was passed directly from the donor to the patient, the blood would clot. It could not be stored for any length

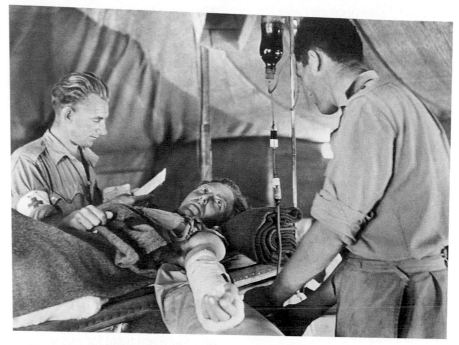

« **Since the 1940s, blood transfusions have become common** »

of time. During the First World War some anticoagulants were discovered. Anticoagulants are substances, such as sodium citrate, that stop blood from clotting. Blood could now be stored in refrigerators for up to three weeks.

Blood banks

Stored blood was given to injured British soldiers during the last two years of the First World War. In 1937, Dr Bernard Fantus began what he called a 'blood bank' for civilians at a hospital in Chicago, USA. His name for the blood store caught on. Meanwhile Charles Drew was making discoveries that would make blood transfusions more common and easier to carry out.

Drew was an African-American, born in Washington, USA. Despite experiencing racism during his education, he qualified as a doctor in Canada. As a young man he

was also a talented sportsman. He returned to the USA to study and work in New York and became the first black American to be awarded a doctor of science. Drew discovered that if blood plasma was separated from the red blood cells, the plasma could be given to any patient needing blood. Matching blood types was only

« **Karl Landsteiner, the discoverer of blood groups** »

« **Charles Drew, blood bank pioneer** »

needed if haemoglobin was required. This meant that more use could be made of donated blood.

During the Second World War, Drew organised the collection of blood for British soldiers. When the USA joined the war he organised blood banks for the American Red Cross. Drew still faced racism. The American Medical Association refused to accept him because he was black, and the USA War Department told the Red Cross to separate the blood of black donors from that of white donors. Drew resigned, as he knew that there was no difference in the blood of different races.

Refusing blood

Most religious groups have changed their attitude to blood transfusions in the last 300 years. While blood may still be important to their beliefs, they no longer see a problem in one person donating their blood to save the life of another. But one group, the Jehovah's Witnesses still believe it is wrong for the blood of one person to be given to another. There have been occasions when Jehovah's Witnesses have refused blood for themselves or even their children despite losing a lot of blood. They have refused life-saving operations because they involved blood transfusions. Doctors and hospitals have even been to court to get permission to give blood to the children of Jehovah's Witnesses.

Doctor's who sympathise with Jehovah's Witnesses have tried to find ways round the problem. They have found methods of carrying out operations without loss of blood. Recently the Jehovah's

Witnesses have accepted transfusions of substances that can replace blood but not the whole blood taken from another person. An example is a form of haemoglobin, the oxygen-carrying compound, obtained from cow's blood.

Contamination

For many people receiving a blood transfusion has meant that their life can continue as normal. Sometimes there are worries that the blood they have been given may be contaminated by diseases. Blood donors have to be healthy and there are tests for many infectious diseases carried by blood. Disasters do happen, however.

In the early 1980s, some people were found to have developed AIDS after receiving blood. At that time the cause of AIDS was unknown and hundreds were infected before something could be done. In 1985, a test was developed which could show if the donor was carrying the HIV virus,

which causes AIDS. People who tested positive were no longer allowed to donate blood.

Blood substitutes

Transfusions of whole blood were unsuccessful before Landsteiner discovered blood types and doctors tried to use other liquids as substitutes for blood. In the 1880s, it was discovered that salt solution could be injected into the blood without ill effect. Although the salt solution could replace fluid in the body it couldn't carry oxygen, the blood's main function. The search went on for a substitute.

Today the need for a substitute is even more pressing. The demand for blood is huge and there is a struggle to find enough suitable donors. There are two possible solutions to the problem.

Haemoglobin can be taken from other creatures and chemically altered so that it can be injected into humans. As the altered haemoglobin is pure it cannot

BSE and vCJD are diseases similar to each other, which cause a breakdown of nerve cells in the brain. The brain becomes spongy as the holes grow and less able to function.

In the late 1990s, there was a scare about BSE. Some people thought that the substances that cause the human form of BSE, vCJD, could be passed on through blood transfusions. There is no evidence to show that anyone has ever been infected with vCJD from blood transfusions. No evidence does not mean there is proof however. No way of testing donors' blood for vCJD has yet been found. The only way that the blood transfusion service can reduce the risk is to prevent people who live with, or are related to, vCJD sufferers, from donating blood.

pass on diseases. It can also be stored for longer than whole blood.

The other possibility is a totally artificial blood substitute. Compounds of fluorine and carbon, called fluorocarbons, absorb oxygen in a similar way to haemoglobin. Mice will happily swim submerged in a bath of fluorocarbon and rats have had their blood swapped for fluorocarbon. Tests are being done to see if the artificial blood is safe and suitable for use in humans. ■

« This mouse is breathing oxygen dissolved in the fluorocarbon it is swimming in »

« Blood is stored for a few weeks »

The bar chart shows blood stocks on a typical day. The total stock is over 50 000 units of blood. Blood can be kept for up to six weeks. The stock of group O is the largest in the number of units stored because group O blood can be given to any patient.

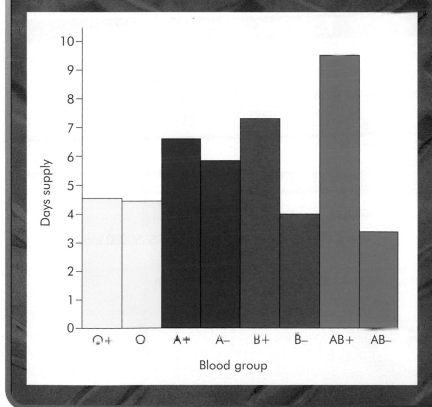

Blood group	Days' supply
O+	4.6
O–	4.5
A+	6.7
A–	5.9
B+	7.3
B–	4.0
AB+	9.6
AB–	3.3

1 Blood from donors can only be stored for about six weeks. This is because blood is a very complicated mixture of substances that deteriorate even when kept cold. What do the different substances in blood do?

2 Find out more about the life and work of either James Blundell, Karl Landsteiner or Charles Drew.

3 Why do you think the USA War Department wanted to keep the blood of black and white people separate during the Second World War? Would you have acted in the same way that Charles Drew did?

4 Some doctors have developed ways of carrying out surgery without loss of blood. Why have these doctors done this?

Discussion

1 Should we be worried about the possibility of getting vCJD by blood transfusions? Discuss the risks and the ways in which contamination could be prevented.

2 In Britain blood is only taken from volunteer donors. In some countries donors are paid for their blood. Discuss the arguments for and against paying donors.

3 If you lived at the time of Jean Baptiste Denis' experiment, would you support further experiments or the ban on transfusions?

Extra activities

Imagine you were a newspaper or TV journalist in France in 1668. Write an article including interviews with Jean Baptiste Denis, the gaolers, and members of the government, the church and the public. What were their thoughts about Denis' experiment on Mauroy?

WEBSITES

http://www.blood.co.uk/welcome.htm

http://encarta.msn.com/index/conciseindex/55/05550000.htm?z=1&pg=2&br=1

http://www.watchtower.org/library/hb/index.htm

Pumping heart

15/07/2018 *TimesNet World News:*
New hearts for old

Kate Matthews, a 45-year old online dream synthesiser, has become the first person to receive a transplant of her own heart tissue. Robo surgeons at a London hospital carried out the four-hour operation earlier today.

The heart tissue was grown from stem cells removed from Ms Matthews's bone marrow a few months ago. Diseased heart tissue was removed and the new muscle transplanted to take its place.

Ms Matthews is said to have recovered consciousness and her new heart is performing well. She is expected to make a speedy recovery and will not need immunity-suppressing drugs as her body will recognise the new tissue as her own.

Stem cells are present in embryos and some adult tissues. They have the ability to develop into any tissue in the body. Research on the use of stem cells in medicine began in the 1990s, but only since 2012 has it been possible to grow human organs from adult stem cells. Growing their own heart means that patients no longer need a donor. The new technique will provide competition for the artificial hearts that have been in use for over 20 years.

20/03/2002 *The News*
Two-year-old receives artificial heart

Emile Jutras yesterday became the youngest person to be fitted with an artificial heart. Two-year-old Emile was born with a heart defect, which means that he must have a heart transplant as soon as possible. The mechanical pump will assist his own heart until a suitable donor is found. Dr Renzo Cecere at Montreal Hospital said that the operation was a complete success.

Mechanical pumps can replace the human heart

The use of artificial hearts has become common in recent years. Early versions used in the 1980s were not successful because blood clotting lead to fatal strokes. The new pumps produce a continuous flow of about four litres per minute without a pulse. Their on-board batteries can be charged through the skin. They are made of new materials which do not cause clotting. It is estimated that about 50 000 people in the USA need a heart transplant every year. There are only about 7000 potential donors, so demand for artificial hearts could be huge.

04/12/1967
The Daily Reporter
Man given heart of woman

Louis Washkansky yesterday became the first living person to have his heart removed and replaced by another. Dr Christian Barnard carried out the operation at a Cape Town hospital. The heart donor, Denise Darrall was killed in a car crash. Mr Washkansky has been given drugs which will stop his body rejecting his new heart. He is awake and doing well, his doctors report.

Mr Washkansky died 18 days later from pneumonia. The drugs had made it easy for infections to take hold. Nevertheless the success of the operation showed that heart transplants were possible. In the next 30 years heart transplantation became a frequent operation carried out across the world. Now heart transplant patients can expect to live a normal life so long as they take the anti-rejection drugs and avoid infections.

Spare part surgery

Since 1967, swapping a diseased heart for a replacement has become almost normal. Hearts are taken from people who have died in accidents or from diseases that do not affect the heart. Today, artificial hearts of plastic and metal are starting to be used. Perhaps in the future grow-your-own heart tissue will become a reality. Hearts grown by genetically modified pigs are also a possibility. If you have a problem with your heart, unplug the old one and plug in a new one.

Where did this idea of the heart as an interchangeable mechanical pump come from? For the answer we have to go back nearly 400 years and meet William Harvey.

AN UNLIKELY REVOLUTIONARY

William Harvey was born in Folkestone in Kent in 1578. His wealthy landowner father paid for him to go to Cambridge University, where he studied the arts and medicine. He decided to become a medical doctor. To complete his training he went to the most famous medical college of the time in Padua, Italy. He returned to England in 1602 and began his medical practice. The nobility became his patients and in 1618 he became doctor to King James I and then King Charles I. While the Civil War between King and Parliament raged, Harvey supported the King spending most of his time at Oxford, the Royalist stronghold. When Oxford fell to Cromwell and Parliament, in 1646, Harvey took the opportunity to retire. He died in 1657.

William Harvey carried out experiments to test his ideas on circulation of the blood

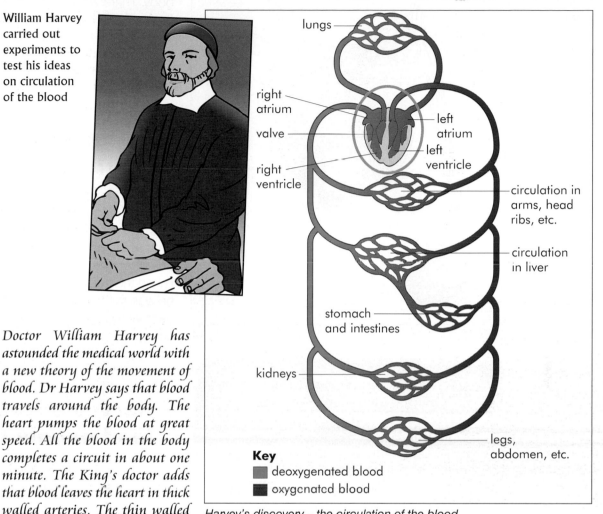

Harvey's discovery – the circulation of the blood

Key
- deoxygenated blood
- oxygenated blood

Doctor William Harvey has astounded the medical world with a new theory of the movement of blood. Dr Harvey says that blood travels around the body. The heart pumps the blood at great speed. All the blood in the body completes a circuit in about one minute. The King's doctor adds that blood leaves the heart in thick walled arteries. The thin walled veins contain flaps of tissue which act as valves and make the blood move only towards the heart. Dr Harvey's ideas have been published in a book that is known as **Du Motu Cordis** (the movement of the heart).

The response to Dr Harvey's ideas has been mixed. Many say that the teachings of Aristotle and the Roman hero of medicine, Galen, will not be forgotten quickly. Others say that Harvey's theory shows the body to be simply a machine. The heart is just a pump supplying blood to all parts of the body and not the centre of emotions that it was thought to be.

Before Harvey

At Cambridge and Padua, Harvey had been taught the ideas of the ancient philosophers, Aristotle and Galen. Aristotle thought that the heart was where feelings such as happiness, sadness and love were felt. That is why we send cards covered with hearts on Valentine's Day.

Galen, a Roman doctor, looked at the bodies of animals but was not allowed to dissect human bodies. He decided that there were two types of blood. One type was made in the liver and passed through the heart, and then through the veins to the rest of the body. The second type of blood came from the lungs where air had given it life. This blood also passed

Aristotle thought that the heart was where feelings such as happiness, sadness and love were felt.

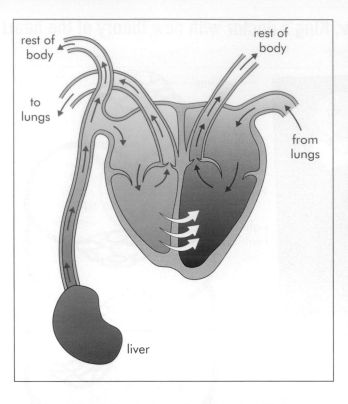

« Galen's model of the heart. Note the blood moving through the central wall of the heart »

rest of body

rest of body

to lungs

from lungs

liver

through the heart and was carried by the arteries to the rest of the body. There was no circulation, the flow was slow and the heart did little but heat the blood. The two types of blood were largely kept separate. A small volume of blood was thought to pass through pores in the central wall of the heart.

Harvey – modern scientist?

Harvey's ideas changed the way people thought about the body. He was right about the blood moving around the body although he was unable to see the capillaries that linked the arteries to the veins and he was right about the way the heart acted. But was he a modern scientist?

What Harvey did

- He dissected bodies to see the connections between the heart, arteries and veins.

- Harvey observed the bodies of deer killed on a hunt. He saw that when a vein was cut, blood did not flow out from the end leading to the heart.

- He saw that veins contained flaps of tissue that acted as valves. Blood can only travel along veins towards the heart. Arteries have no valves.

- He watched the beating hearts of living animals. He estimated how much blood was passed out of the heart on each pumping action. (For a man it worked out to be about four litres a minute.)

- Harvey bound a cord around his upper arm. He noted that his veins swelled and he could still feel a pulse in his arm. Blood flowed through the arteries of his arm and into his veins but was stopped from returning to his heart.

- When he tied the cord tightly, his veins did not swell and the pulse stopped. Now, blood could not pass through the arteries of his arm.

- He showed that there was no connection between the two sides of the heart.

Harvey's ideas lead people to think of the body as a machine.

Although Harvey turned the heart into a simple pump, he agreed with Aristotle in many ways. In his book he refers to Aristotle's idea of the Sun warming the oceans to start the water cycle. In the same way he says, the heart warms the blood and drives it around the body. He also uses some of the symbolic language of the ancient art of alchemy to describe what happens to the blood during its circuit.

Harvey carried out experiments but unlike Galileo he didn't make accurate measurements. The amount of blood pumped by the heart on each beat was a guess.

Harvey's ideas lead people to think of the body as a machine. Each organ had its task in ensuring that the whole machine worked, in the same way that the processor, hard drive, display screen and keyboard form a computer system. Harvey didn't see it this way. He thought the blood was alive and that the heart pumped because that was what it was made to do.

So, Harvey stands with one foot in the old world of the philosophers and the other in modern science. It was his successors who developed his ideas and set medicine on the path to heart transplants. ∎

Questions

1 There is a shortage of suitable donors for heart transplants as well as other organs. Why is this? What could be done to encourage more donors?

2 In the future there may be a choice of at least four ways of replacing a damaged heart. What are the four methods mentioned in this article? Which do you think is likely to be the most important?

3 One of the ideas that William Harvey learnt from his teachers was that the heart is where emotions form. Think of examples of how that idea still exists in the way we talk today.

4 Harvey carried out experiments on live animals. It is known as vivisection. Why was this important in finding out how the heart worked? Why was it not possible to get the full story by looking at dead bodies?

5 Compare the modern view with the ancient view of circulation, i.e. Harvey versus Galen. How did Harvey's experiments and observations show that Galen was wrong?

Discussion

When the early models of artificial hearts were used in the 1980s, the patients died within weeks or months. The patients knew that their chances of survival were small. Is this type of experimentation justified? What would you say if you were suffering a terminal disease and were asked to take part in a similar experiment?

Extra activities

It is nearly 40 years since the first heart transplant. Find out about someone who has had a heart transplant. How has it changed their life?

Seeing clearly

Do you wear glasses or contact lenses? If you do, you are in good company, as about half of the people you meet will wear glasses or contact lenses at least some of the time.

It may seem strange that half the population seems to have something wrong with their eyes. It could be that our lifestyle has caused eye problems. Some people think that making children wear glasses while they are growing actually makes the problems worse.

So why do we wear glasses?

Short and long sight

Eyes are like a camera. When light enters the eye or a camera it is bent to form an image. In the camera the lens bends the light. In the eye the same job is done by a lens and the cornea. The cornea is the clear, curved surface over the front of the eye. The cornea does most of the light bending. The lens changes shape to make sure that near and distant objects can be seen clearly. If the shape of the cornea and the eye is not right then a sharp image cannot be formed.

If the light is bent too much, the image forms in front of the retina.

This is called short sight. A short-sighted person has trouble seeing distant objects.

If the light is not bent enough, the rays of light do not meet. The

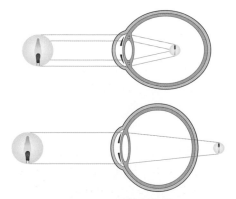

« **If the eye is the wrong shape a sharp image does not fall on the retina** »

image would form behind the retina. This is called long sight. Long-sighted people cannot see objects that are close to them clearly. Many people become long-sighted as they get older.

Four-eyes

The Chinese may have invented spectacles or glasses two thousand years ago. Glasses appeared in Europe in the 13th century. In 1289, an Italian wrote:

Without the glasses known as spectacles, I would no longer be able to read or write. These have recently been invented for the benefit of poor old people whose sight has become weak.

To correct short sight, concave lenses are used. These are thinner in the middle than at the edge. Convex lenses are used for long sight. Convex lenses are thicker in the middle. Early lenses were made from quartz because the glass that was available was not very clear. Later the quality of glass improved. Various ways of

balancing spectacles on noses were tried out.

Although spectacles were very expensive they soon became important possessions for educated people. Wearing spectacles became a sign of intelligence. No geek goes without his specs. Even Superman wears specs when he's Clark Kent.

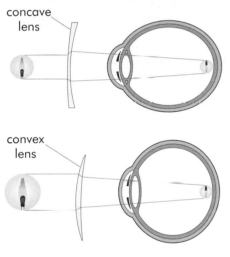

concave lens

convex lens

Contacts

The problems of balancing two heavy glass lenses in front of the eyes made some people look for other ways to cure poor eyesight. Late in the 19th century various people started experimenting with contact lenses – glass lenses that fitted on the eye. Although they were successful, the large size of the early contact lenses made them uncomfortable to wear for long periods.

The small plastic lenses which are available today are much more comfortable to wear. Contacts have become popular, even if

more time has to be spent searching for the lens that has dropped out.

Finding a cure

Wearing glasses or contacts doesn't cure eye problems. Short and long sight are caused by misshapen eyes. To cure the problem the shape of the eye must be changed. Russian surgeons were the first to do operations on eyes to improve long and short sight. Surgeons used a diamond knife to cut parts of the cornea. This changed the way the cornea bent the light that entered the eye.

This kind of eye surgery only became popular when a laser replaced the diamond knife. For people with fairly minor eye problems the laser vaporises parts of the outer layer of the cornea. For more serious problems the outer layer of cornea is lifted off. Then the laser burns away some of the inner tissue. The outer layer is put back and soon heals. Computer programs calculate exactly where the laser must cut to produce the right shape. It is said that nearly 90% of patients no longer need to wear glasses after treatment. The treatment is expensive and costs about £2000 for both eyes. This is about ten times the cost of spectacles.

A warning ⚠️

Not everyone thinks that cutting the cornea with diamonds or

lasers is a good thing. As a person gets older their eyes change. No one really knows what the effect of laser surgery will be after 10 or 20 years. Some doctors fear that the improvements made by laser surgery could be temporary. Cutting the cornea could cause problems later in life.

Alternatives

Perhaps we should just learn to take more care of our eyes. Short sight in children may be made worse if they wear glasses all day long to do school work. Scientists in the USA are experimenting with a drug that stops short-sighted eyes from getting worse. But for now there is no real substitute for specs and contacts. Four eyes are here to stay. ■

Questions

1 Why do you think that educated people found spectacles a valuable invention?

2 What advantages do contact lenses have over spectacles?

3 A short-sighted friend asks for your advice about having laser eye surgery. Describe the arguments for and against having treatment.

4 Describe the contributions scientists have made to help people with short and long sight.

Extra activities

Carry out a survey of eye problems in your class or family. How many people wear spectacles or contact lenses and how many do not need them at all? Are there any patterns? For example, do more people wear spectacles as they get older? Does wearing spectacles run in families? Is short sight or long sight most common?

The Pill

Is it right that perfectly healthy people should take a drug that has a powerful effect on their bodies? No, we're not referring to ecstasy or cannabis, but to the contraceptive pill. Today 100 million women worldwide pop the little pill into their mouths nearly every day so that they can have sex without the fear of becoming pregnant.

The birth of the Pill

Throughout history women have looked for ways to avoid having a baby. Every civilisation has devised contraceptive methods, some more weird than successful. The most reliable method of stopping the sperm reach the egg is the condom or sheath, but it is the man's duty to wear it. Until 1960, women had few methods in their control that they could rely on. One of the pioneers of the birth control movement in the USA, Margaret Sanger, knew all about women's needs. She saw the health of women destroyed by repeated pregnancies. Women came to her pioneering clinic appealing for help so that they could avoid having more children.

« Margaret Sanger, birth control pioneer »

In the late 1940s, Katharine McCormick, a wealthy heiress, offered Margaret Sanger help to pay for research into contraception. The sponsorship went to Gregory Pincus who in 1944 was one of the founders of the Worcester Foundation for Experimental Biology in Massachusetts.

Pincus was born in New Jersey in 1903 and was an expert on female hormones and the human egg. He began to look for ways in which the female menstrual cycle could be tampered with to prevent pregnancy. Pincus was aware of the work of Russell Marker.

Russell Marker was a chemist who had discovered how to turn compounds called steroids, found in plants, into human hormones. Marker had had battles with his superiors at Pennsylvania State

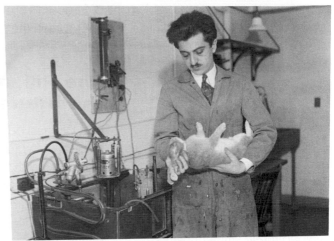

« The fathers of the pill? Carl Djerassi and Gregory Pincus »

University and left to set up his own company, Syntex, in Mexico City. His first success was to make cortisone, a steroid used to treat arthritis. In 1949, Marker employed Carl Djerassi to work on female hormones.

Djerassi was born in 1913, in Vienna where his parents were doctors. In 1938, his life was in danger from the Nazis because he was a Jew. He fled to the USA. Djerassi was soon recognised as an expert chemist but made a bold move to leave the USA for Mexico City. By 1951, he had succeeded in synthesising a form of progesterone, one of the menstrual hormones. The starting point was a steroid found in the roots of Mexican yams. It was thought that the drug would be useful in treating women with period problems.

Meanwhile at the larger drug company, G.D. Searle, Frank Colton had made the same discovery. Colton was another refugee, having been born in Poland in 1923. Like Djerassi, Colton thought that his product might have some use helping women with their periods.

Gregory Pincus realised that the substance that Djerassi and

Colton had made could act as a contraceptive. He carried out tests on women in Massachusetts, Puerto Rico and Haiti using Colton's product, which was called Enovid. By 1955, Pincus had the results. Enovid was a very reliable contraceptive with apparently little or no side effects. Marker's company, Syntex, also carried out trials of Djerassi's product and found it was a good contraceptive

In 1960, the American Food and Drug Administration approved the use of both Searle's and Syntex's contraceptive pills. At first the Pill was only available to married women, particularly those who

were thought to be in danger if they had another pregnancy. Soon many more women, married and single, clamoured for the Pill. At last they had control over when and if they became pregnant. The availability of the Pill helped to make the 60s 'swing' and encouraged people to think that casual sex was safe.

Scares and risks

The contraceptive pill developed by Djerassi and Colton contained a mixture of oestrogen and progesterone, two hormones that played a big part in the early stages of pregnancy. Early trials

« The pill helped to make the 60s swing »

suggested there were no problems for women taking the Pill, but this was in the days before thalidomide.

Thalidomide was a drug given to pregnant women to ease morning sickness. Unfortunately a side effect was that many children were born with serious deformities. Following the thalidomide disaster, new drugs had to go through many more tests and trials. The Pill avoided these stricter checks.

Luckily the Pill didn't have as dramatic a side effect as thalidomide but as the years passed evidence of problems started to collect. Some women taking the Pill suffered from thrombosis – blood clots in the heart, lungs or brain. These could be fatal.

Then in the 1980s large-scale surveys of women showed that, if they had been taking the Pill for at least eight years, they had an increased risk of breast cancer. The risk was greatest in women who started taking the Pill when they were in their teens. The solution seemed to be to reduce the strength of the hormones in the Pill. The amount of oestrogen was reduced by 40% and the amount of progesterone by 90%. A 'mini-pill' containing no oestrogen at all was developed. It may protect women from cancer of the ovaries but is less effective as a contraceptive.

Newspaper and TV reports of the risks scared many women. The number taking the Pill dropped for a time. They were told that the new low-dose pills would not affect health and soon the sale of the Pill rose again. Today the business is worth $2.9 billion a year. For women taking the Pill, the benefits

of freedom from pregnancy seem to outweigh the unproved but well-publicised health risks.

The Pill, AIDs and the future

Carl Djerassi became one of the leaders of Syntex and made a fortune from its business. In 1959 he moved to Stanford University in California and continued his biochemical work. He also became a celebrity, appearing on TV programmes to discuss the Pill and its effects on society.

One thing that Djerassi and sociologists did not foresee was the coming of the AIDS epidemic. The Pill provides no protection against the disease for women. A condom is necessary for safe sex. Once again women no longer have full control over their bodies.

Djerassi also observes that there has been more research done to help women have children than on the contraceptive pill. Now, he says, a safer and more reliable alternative to the Pill would be for men to give a sample to a sperm bank and then have a vasectomy. When a woman wants a baby she

could then collect sperm from the bank. There have been trials of contraceptive pills for men, but for now it is still the woman who must pop a pill every night. ∎

Questions

1 Why was the contraceptive pill at first only available to married women?

2 Gregory Pincus died in 1967 while Carl Djerassi is still often in the public eye because of the 'science-in-fiction' novels that he has written since he retired from research. Djerassi and Pincus have each been called the father of the Pill. Do you think either deserves this title? Was the contribution of Margaret Sanger or Frank Colton as important?

3 If the Pill had gone through the post-thalidomide checks it may not have been made available so easily. How do you think this may have changed people's attitude to the Pill and sex?

4 Are the health risks of the Pill greater than the benefits of its contraceptive effects?

Discussion

1 The Pill was intended originally to help women with problems with their periods. Discuss whether you think it is right that the drug should be freely available to women who do not have such problems.

2 The Pill works in two ways. One is to stop the woman's egg being released from the ovaries. The second prevents a fertilised egg from attaching to the wall of the womb. Some people say that life begins once the egg has been fertilised. How would you respond to someone who said that taking the Pill was a form of abortion and should not be allowed?

3 Some people think that the Pill has caused a big change in the way people think about having sex. What do you think? Are the changes for the better of for worse?

SICK TO DEATH

Floods bring disease

Flood water spreads microbes that cause diseases

Risk of disease for earthquake survivors

Earthquake destroys sewers and water pipes. Survivors are likely to catch diseases.

Refugees of war face disease

Refugees are weak from lack of food. Living close together spreads disease.

How often have you seen newspaper headlines like these following a disaster or war in some far-off country? When civilisation breaks down people begin to suffer from a wide range of diseases. It is not only a problem for developing countries. After the widespread floods in Britain in the autumn of 2000 there were warnings about the risk of disease. Flood water may have got into the fresh water supply.

However it is the developing countries that face the greatest risk of disease as a result of natural and man-made disasters. Cholera, typhoid and diseases caused by poor diet are often found among populations thrown out of their homes.

Living with disease

For many people in developing countries, living with the threat of disease is the normal way of life. Cholera, typhoid, bilharzia, malaria and tuberculosis are just some of the diseases caused by bacteria and viruses that threaten people every day of their lives. In addition there are the diseases caused by poor diet such as beri-beri, and there is also the new threat of AIDS.

In the prosperous countries of the world, disease is different. Here people suffer from what may be called lifestyle diseases, such as heart disease and lung cancer. But the old infectious diseases cannot be forgotten. Foreign travel brings people into contact with infections, which they can spread on their return home. Resistance to antibiotics is causing diseases such as tuberculosis (TB) to become common again. Climate change could widen the range of some disease-carrying organisms like the malaria mosquito.

Clean water and sewers

Some of the greatest achievements of Victorian engineers in British cities were the building of water supplies and sanitation systems. The growing population of the industrial cities at last had access to clean water. Their waste was kept away from the water supply so that drinking water could not be contaminated by faeces. Elsewhere in Europe and North America similar improvements during the 19th and early 20th centuries improved the health of the population. Now nearly everyone in the developed world has clean water running from a tap and a flush toilet to dispose of waste. It is not the same in the developing world. The table shows the situation in just a few developing countries:

DR SNOW AND THE CHOLERA OUTBREAK

Cholera was one of the first diseases to be studied and controlled. Epidemics were frequent during the 19th century. On the 31st August 1854 some people started showing the symptoms of cholera in the Soho area of London. They became feverish and suffered from diarrhoea. In just four days over 100 people were dead.

Dr John Snow, a surgeon who lived nearby, was concerned by the epidemic. He studied a map of the area on which he marked every case – over 500 of them. Most people thought that cholera and other diseases were caused by the foul-smelling air of the city. Dr Snow had a different idea. He thought there was something in the drinking water that caused the disease. Most of the cases were in the Broad Street area of Soho and Snow realised that they were clustered around one pump that people used as their source of water for drinking, cooking and washing. Snow decided to take action. He spoke to the authorities and they reluctantly allowed him to remove the lever from the hand pump. People could no longer collect the water. The people were furious as they had to travel further to get water, but in days the epidemic was over.

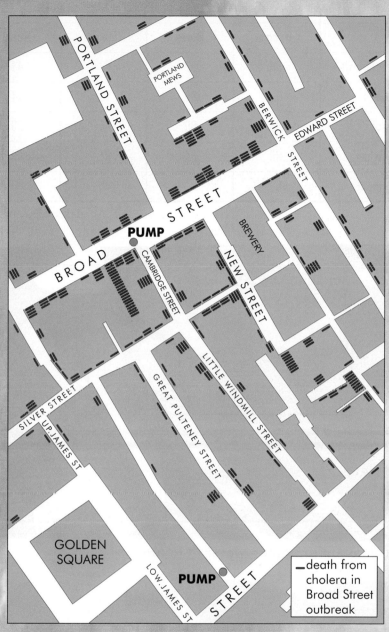

<< The cholera cases logged by Dr John Snow in Soho >>

Some people said that the epidemic was already decreasing when Snow acted, but there were no further cases. Snow had seen the cholera bacterium on a microscope slide of the pump water and felt certain that it was responsible for the disease. Pasteur's work on the germ theory of disease was still some years off and even Snow did not fully understand what was happening. The bacteria multiply rapidly in the gut of infected people and pass out in their faeces. If these wastes mix with water used for drinking or cooking the disease spreads. Eventually the importance of clean water was recognised.

Country	% of population with access to:			
	Safe water		Sanitation	
	Urban	Rural	Urban	Rural
Bangladesh	99	97	82	44
India	92	86	73	14
Nepal	85	80	75	20
Pakistan	96	84	94	42
Singapore	100	–	100	–

Source: Asian Development Bank.

« **This plant produces water fit to drink** »

« **In many shanty towns waste runs in open sewers** »

Typhoid

Typhoid is a bacterial disease found where water supplies and sanitation are poor or damaged. Over 12 million people a year suffer from typhoid worldwide. The disease causes a fever, stomach pains, headache and sometimes a rash, but mysteriously sometimes it produces no symptoms at all. People can become carriers of the typhoid bacteria and bring it to areas that were clear of the disease. If a person is unaware that he/she is a carrier, they can pass it on by contact with other people or when preparing food (see the story of Typhoid Mary in the Key Stage 3 *Science Web Reader Biology*, published by Nelson Thornes).

Typhoid is one of the diseases feared most when a disaster strikes and people are unable to use hygienic methods of preparing food. However, unlike cholera, there is an effective vaccination for typhoid.

Bilharzia

Bilharzia is a disease that affects the millions of people who live in rural tropical areas. It is not caused by a microbe but is due to a tiny parasitic worm. The worm emerges from water snails into the ponds and streams that people use for washing and fishing. The worms set up home in human veins and spend their time producing millions of eggs. The eggs are released in urine and faeces. The problem continues because in many rural areas the sewage containing the eggs ends up in the ponds and streams. The eggs hatch into larva which attack the water snails and the cycle is repeated. Over 300 million people suffer from the anaemia and fatigue that the worms cause.

The solution is to break the worm's life cycle. One way is to destroy the

Over 300 million people suffer from the anaemia and fatigue that the worms cause.

habitats of the snails, but a better way is to prevent the human waste from mixing with the clean water.

Tuberculosis (TB)

There are many stories of people with 'consumption' in the 19th and early 20th centuries. Sufferers slowly weakened and finally died from the lung disease. Some lived their lives in isolation hospitals while those who could afford it moved to countries with a better climate. The modern name for consumption is tuberculosis or TB. In the developed countries a programme of testing and treatment with antibiotics seemed to get the disease under control and at the end of the 20th century it was an uncommon disease. But diseases rarely disappear completely.

Elsewhere in the world TB is anything but uncommon. Millions of people suffer from the disease in countries where families live in single rooms or huddle together in shanty towns. In these places medical care is very limited. TB victims cough repeatedly, constantly feel tired, lose weight and appetite, have a fever and cough up blood. Finally they are killed by the bacteria. Many millions more are carriers of the disease but are unaffected by it.

TB is actually quite a difficult disease to catch. You have to be very close to someone who is carrying the bacteria in order to be infected. Nevertheless in just the continent of Africa it is thought that over a billion people will become infected in the next 20 years with over 200 million falling sick.

There are drugs to cope with the disease but they are expensive. If

In 1887, Christiaan Eijkman observed the effects of beri-beri in an army camp. The main food of the soldiers was processed or 'polished' rice. He noticed that the chickens which ate the leftovers also suffered from beri-beri. When the chickens were moved and fed on untreated rice they recovered. Eijkman decided that there was something wrong with the polished rice the soldiers were eating and substituted untreated rice. They soon recovered. The germ theory of disease was the new idea at the time so Eijkman thought beri-beri was caused by bacteria that had contaminated the treated rice. It was not until 1912 that Casimir Funk realised that it was something missing from polished rice that caused the disease. He identified the essential substance that maintained good health as a 'vitamin'. For beri-beri, the vitamin needed was thiamine or B_1. The vitamin forms part of the husk of the rice seed, which is removed from 'polished' rice.

« Christiaan Eijkman and Casimir Funk »

« Chopin suffered from consumption, which is now known as TB »

sufferers do not complete a course of drugs the bacteria becomes resistant and the patient falls sick again. Now resistant strains of bacteria are causing the spread of the disease in countries where it hasn't been a problem for decades. TB is back.

Malnutrition

Famine is a constant threat for people who rely on their land for food. War and disaster can disrupt their farming. But sometimes even when there is apparently sufficient food, people may suffer from diseases caused by something missing from their diet. One such disease is beri-beri. The missing substance is thiamine or vitamin B_1, found in the husk of the rice seed. The symptoms of the disease are loss of weight, tiredness and loss of appetite. The disease was once common in many parts of the world but particularly in the Far East.

If other vitamins are missing from diets, different diseases occur. For example, if vitamin C is missing from people's diets they suffer from scurvy, while a lack of vitamin D causes the bone disease, rickets.

In all parts of the world, poor people who cannot afford a balanced diet are likely to suffer from deficiency diseases. ■

Questions

1 Some diseases are caused by microbes (bacteria and viruses), others by parasites, and others by poor diets. What are the causes of the following diseases: beri-beri, typhoid, bilharzia, scurvy, cholera, tuberculosis?

2 Cases of cholera are very rare in Britain. Explain why.

3 Dr John Snow is now seen as something of a hero but few people listened to his ideas in the 1850s. Why was this?

4 Advice is often given to tourists visiting countries where cholera and typhoid occur: 'When preparing food – cook it, peel it or forget it.' Explain why this is a sensible warning.

5 Look at the table on page 27.
   a) Of the countries listed, which has the biggest percentage of its population without proper sanitation?
   b) Why is safe water and sanitation more available in urban areas?
   c) Although urban areas have higher rates of safe water and sanitation, why are epidemics of diseases more likely in cities?
   d) The whole of the population of Singapore has access to safe water and sanitation. Why has Singapore been able to achieve this?

6 In some cities in Europe and North America rates of tuberculosis infection have increased. What reasons can you give for this?

7 In some places where people suffer from TB, patients are not allowed to simply purchase a supply of the antibiotics. Instead, medical workers ensure that the patients take the drugs every day until the course of treatment is complete. Why do they do this?

8 Why do you think that Christiaan Eijkman thought that beri-beri was caused by a bacterium?

9 Find out the symptoms of scurvy and rickets.

Extra activities

1 An earthquake has devastated a Pacific island. Roads, electricity and water supply lines have been broken. Within days people are starting to fall ill. You are the leader of a relief team sent to help the population. What do you do?

2 Polished rice is easier to cook and some people prefer its taste to untreated rice. Design a poster warning people of the dangers of beri-beri.

@ WEBSITES @

http://news.bbc.co.uk

http://www.adb.org

Smoking

counting the risks

We have all seen these messages on cigarette advertising boards and health leaflets but do they have any effect? All the gruesome pictures of diseased, tar-filled lungs and wheezing old men does not seem to stop many people from smoking. In fact the number of young women smoking has actually increased. While smokers are banned from public buildings and offices, the tobacco companies still do business, governments collect the tax and some sports go on accepting millions of pounds in sponsorship. What is the story behind the tobacco controversy?

The killer strikes

During the 1930s and 1940s, doctors in Europe and America noticed an increase in the number

« The original government health warning »

« ... the new warning. No excuse for ignoring it! »

of people dying from lung cancer. In Britain, the medical authorities became especially worried after the Second World War, as the death toll seemed to be growing fast. Austin Bradford Hill, a leading epidemiologist (someone who looks for patterns of disease in populations), was asked to investigate. Hill invited the young Richard Doll to join the study.

In 1948, they began interviewing lung cancer patients and fit people living in London. Although some doctors had thought that smoking might be a cause of ill health, most dismissed the idea. Richard Doll thought that the cause of lung cancer might be the smoky exhausts of cars and lorries, which were beginning to clog the roads in the cities. By 1949, the results of the survey became clear.

The link between the lung cancer patients was how much they had smoked. Smokers seemed to have an increased chance of getting lung cancer. Of course not all the lung cancer patients were smokers and many of the fit people did smoke, but analysis of the data using statistics showed up the link. Hill and Doll were still unsure about their conclusions. Perhaps there was something peculiar to London. They expanded their study to include Newcastle, Bristol, Leeds and Cambridge, with the same results. They published their report in September 1950.

Meanwhile in the USA, Ernst Wynder had carried out a similar survey and also found a link between smoking and lung cancer, which he published in May 1950.

The controversy begins

The publication of Hill and Doll's work in Britain and Wynder's in the USA did not have much effect straight away. Many doctors and scientists did not believe that such a common habit as smoking could have such serious health effects. They said that the surveys only showed that some people who had lung cancer had smoked. Neither Doll nor Wynder had suggested how smoking caused cancers. Tests had been done to see if tobacco tar caused cancers in animals but the results had proved negative. Richard Doll realised that the tests had not been done for a long enough period of time.

In 1953, the British government set up a committee to look at the studies that had been done. The committee decided that there was a link between smoking and lung cancer. In the USA, where a lot of tobacco is grown, the government did not accept the results. Wynder was ignored by his colleagues.

Doctors thought it unwise to warn people. At the time there was little that could be done to help sufferers of lung cancer. Doctors thought that people would be scared if the news leaked out that smoking was dangerous.

Doll carried out another study in 1954 and an even bigger one in 1956. Each survey showed the link between cancer and smoking.

The tobacco companies fight back

People began to take notice as the conclusions were publicised in 1953. The tobacco companies noticed a small drop in sales. They responded quickly. In 1954, the Tobacco Industry Research Council was set up with funds from the cigarette companies. The TIRC first tried to disprove the findings then offered smokers ways of continuing their habit 'safely'. Filter-tipped cigarettes and low-tar varieties were advertised widely as the safer way to smoke.

The TIRC argued against every new survey. Either they produced a different conclusion or they disputed the way the investigation had been carried out.

The evidence mounts

Richard Doll and other teams across the world continued to collect data showing that smoking was harmful. A heavy smoker has 20 to 30 times more chance of getting lung cancer than a non-smoker. Smoking is the cause of nearly 90% of all lung cancer deaths. The studies also showed that lung cancer wasn't the only health problem caused by smoking. Cancers of the bladder, mouth and throat could all be traced back to tobacco. In fact smoking was found to be responsible for one-third of all male and one-tenth of female deaths due to cancer. Other diseases, particularly of the heart and blood circulation system, were shown to have links with smoking.

In 1964, the Surgeon General in the USA finally had to announce that there was a definite link between smoking and various diseases.

Laboratory tests also proved that substances present in tobacco tar could cause cancers in animals. Cigarettes also produce a lot of carbon monoxide, which damages blood cells. More recent experiments can link substances only found in tobacco to particular cancers.

In 1993, Richard Doll completed a forty-year survey of 34 000 doctors. Half of those who were heavy smokers when they were 35 were dead by the age of 70. Only 20% of non-smokers had died before the same age.

The fight against smoking

The evidence against smoking was clear, but people had to be informed. In the late 1960s, warnings appeared in newspapers and on TV. In the early 1970s, cigarette advertising was banned from TV although adverts for cigars and pipe tobacco continued to be allowed for some years.

≪ Smoking is banned in many public buildings ≫

The chances of a child getting cancer increases if their father is a smoker. About 15% of childhood cancers have been shown to be as a result of the father's smoking. It seems that the DNA in the smoker's sperm is damaged. The damage is carried into the embryo and results in cancers as the child grows.

Governments increased the tax on tobacco. The hope was that people would be put off by the increase in price, but in fact it became a very good source of revenue for the governments.

Tobacco companies were told to put warnings on the packets and in their advertisements. At first these were in small print and only hinted at the dangers. As time went by the companies were forced to make the warnings clearer.

Non-smokers began to demand the right to breathe smoke-free air, particularly when passive smoking was also linked to ill health. ASH (Action on Smoking and Health) was formed to fight for non-smokers. They gradually had success as public buildings, transport and places where people work became smoke-free zones.

People suffering from smoking related illnesses started to take the tobacco companies to court for damages. At first these cases were unsuccessful. The tobacco companies had unlimited amounts of money to spend on lawyers. The cases collapsed because the patient could not prove that their particular cancer could only have been caused by smoking. There are many other causes of cancer that may have been involved. It wasn't until the late 1990s that the tobacco company Philip Morris was forced into paying a huge amount of money to cancer sufferers.

Still smoking

And yet despite all the publicity, tobacco in all its forms still sells. The 1980s and early 1990s showed a steady fall in cigarette sales but more recent data shows that the trend has reversed. Young people are most likely to take up smoking.

The tobacco companies are still huge successful businesses. They

From ritual to habit

« Smoking tobacco was an ancient ritual for native Americans »

When Christopher Columbus arrived in the Caribbean in 1492, he found the native Americans inhaling smoke from the burning leaves of the tobacco plant. Smoking was a ritual at special meetings and celebrations. By the 1550s, the dried leaves had been brought back to Europe and wealthy people were experiencing the pleasant effects of smoking. In the 18th century, pipe smoking and 'taking snuff' became popular.

Cigarettes were developed for women, as a more delicate way of smoking tobacco. In the USA, smoking increased after the Civil War and especially after the invention of the cigarette making machine in 1880. Cigarettes became cheaper and for many people smoking became a habit rather than a special treat. They were encouraged by advertising and even by governments. In the First and Second World Wars cigarettes were supplied free to soldiers, sailors and airmen. By the late 1940s, 85% of middle-aged British men smoked.

Smoking may be good for you

Some studies, like those done by Richard Doll in the 1950s, have shown a link between smoking and brain diseases such as Parkinson's and Alzheimer's. The difference is that smoking may help to prevent these diseases. Scientists are still arguing about whether the results are correct. It has been surprisingly difficult for scientists to get funds to test the benefits of smoking. Perhaps governments are afraid of blurring the picture of smoking being bad for you. Richard Doll thinks that if any benefit of smoking exists it is very small. The risk of getting a cancer is very much greater.

direct their marketing at those that want cigarettes, such as young people. They look for new markets, such as the Far East, where sales can be increased.

Organisations such as FOREST (Freedom Organisation for the Right to Enjoy Smoking Tobacco) campaign for the rights of smokers. In the same way that people may drink alcohol or drive fast cars, smoking is a risk that people can choose for themselves. Why shouldn't people be allowed to smoke if they wish? ■

SIR RICHARD DOLL

Richard Doll was born in 1913 and soon showed that he was keen on maths. He wanted to study maths at Cambridge University but his father was rather short of money and wanted him to study medicine instead. Richard had to win a

« Sir Richard Doll found the link between smoking and cancer »

scholarship if he was to study maths. The night before his last exam at Cambridge he was entertained with some of the very strong college beer. He didn't feel very well the following morning and performed poorly in the exam. Richard lost the scholarship and decided to do as his father wished. He studied medicine at St Thomas's Hospital in London.

Richard's interest in maths didn't disappear. He entered a branch of medicine called epidemiology. This involves looking for patterns of disease in populations. He was soon gaining a reputation as an expert epidemiologist. As well as the smoking surveys he has been involved in many other controversial studies.

In the 1950s he was asked to look into the effects of low levels of radiation. This followed the testing of hydrogen bombs in the atmosphere. The fallout was detected all around the world. Richard discovered that there was no safe level of radiation. It didn't matter whether the radiation was natural or man-made – there was always some risk of getting cancers, such as leukaemia.

In the 1960s, Richard looked at the effect the new contraceptive pill was having on women. He soon found a link between the pill and various health problems. This caused quite a scare and resulted in a reduction in the drug dose in the pill.

Later in his career, he looked at the link between diet and cancers. He investigated many foods that had been suggested as protecting against one type of cancer or another. Results have not always been clear but Richard thinks that fruit and vitamin C can definitely help prevent some cancers.

At the age of 88, Richard (now Sir) still contributes to the work of the Imperial Cancer Research Fund laboratory in Oxford.

REFERENCES

Smoking study strengthens cancer link (1993) *New Scientist*, **137**, no. 1861, 20th Feb.

Ian Mundell (1993) Peering through the smoke screen, *New Scientist*, **140**, no. 1894, 9th Oct.

Questions

1 How did Richard Doll find the link between smoking and lung cancer?

2 How important was Hill and Doll's publication of 1950?

3 In the early 1950s, scientists working for the tobacco companies were able to argue against Richard Doll's conclusions. Now not even the tobacco companies say that smoking does not have risks. How was the controversy decided?

4 The British government recognised the large risk that smoking caused to health in the 1950s, while it took the US government until 1964. What are the reasons for governments not immediately taking steps to ban the sale of tobacco?

5 Sir Richard Doll has spent his life investigating health risks. Summarise the contribution he has made.

Big business

In the late 19th century many small tobacco companies grew. They began to join together to form large corporations that controlled the growing of the tobacco plants, the treatment of the leaves and sale of the products. One example was Philip Morris, which today is one of the largest tobacco companies worldwide.

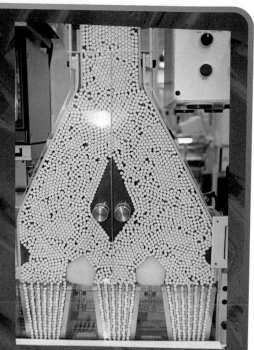

« Cigarette production is big business »

Philip Morris started a tobacco shop in Bond Street, London in the mid-19th century. By the turn of the century his business had grown and he was supplying tobacco to the future King Edward VII. The business saw where its future lay and in 1902 became an American corporation. Soon it was buying and selling tobacco internationally. In the 1950s, the company began to realise that tobacco may become unpopular. It used its wealth to buy other companies in brewing and food production. Today Philip Morris is a huge conglomerate with many products under its control. About 60% of its business is still concerned with tobacco.

A similar story can be told of other tobacco companies. Imperial Tobacco, formed in Britain in 1901 from a lot of smaller companies, has moved into food and dropped 'tobacco' from its name in 1973. British and American Tobacco came into being in 1902 and in 1976 changed its name to BAT Industries plc, with interests in papermaking, department stores and financial services. Despite the changes of name and the variety of interests these companies still deal in tobacco on a huge scale worldwide.

WEBSITES

http://www.philipmorris.com/home.asp

Discussion

1 Much of the work done to prove that tobacco smoke caused cancers was done on animals. Pictures of rabbits forced to inhale through burning cigarettes distressed many people when they were made public. Is the use of animals in this way good science? Discuss and give your reasons for your points of view.

2 Since the 1960s there have been many attempts to try to stop young people from smoking. Sometimes children have been shown gruesome pictures of diseased lungs. Fun days have been organised where the message is repeated over and over again. None of the campaigns has been particularly successful in turning young people off smoking. Discuss why you think so many young people take up smoking?

3 FOREST says people have the right to smoke if they wish. Do you agree? What arguments would you use for and against this statement?

Extra activities

1 Make a list of the many ways in which scientists are involved in the tobacco story.

2 Organise a TV debate between a scientist working for a cancer charity, a representative of ASH, a member of FOREST and a scientist working for a tobacco company. The audience can ask the panel to respond to questions such as
- Does the panel think that tobacco is too dangerous to be used by humans?
- Should spaces in public buildings, such as cinemas and restaurants, be set aside for smokers?
- Are the tobacco companies responsible for the deaths of people who have taken up smoking since warnings were put on cigarette packets?

Pain relief

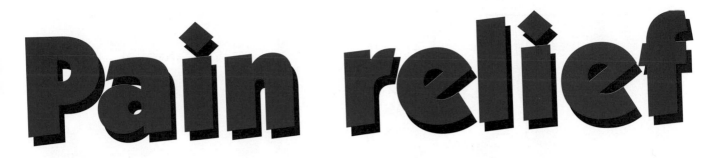

People have always suffered pain. They looked for plants that could ease the pain. The ancient Egyptians found that the opium poppy did the job.

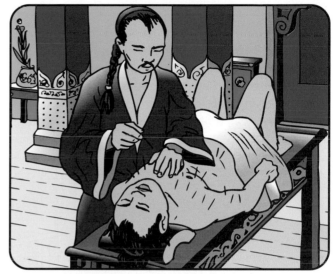

Meanwhile the Chinese invented acupuncture. Needles are inserted into some of the hundreds of points in the 12 pathways of the ch'i. The needles were first made of stone but now metals are used. A patient does not feel any pain even when having an operation.

The Greek doctor, Hippocrates, wrote about a bitter powder obtained from willow bark that could relieve pain. He also used extracts from the opium poppy.

In the Middle Ages the 'soporific sponge' was used for pain relief. The sponge had been boiled in a mixture of opium, nightshade, henbane, hemlock and other powerful extracts from plants. The sponge was moistened and held to the patient's nose.

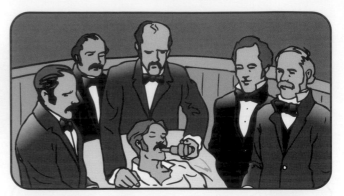

Dr Alex Wood of Edinburgh, invented the needle and syringe in 1843. It was just the thing for injecting morphine into patients with painful illnesses. The German, Friedrich Sertürner had extracted morphine from opium in 1806. Laudanum, a mixture of opium and alcohol, was a favourite painkiller, often used by women.

Humphry Davy suggested that dentists could use the gas called nitrous oxide to deaden the pain caused by rotten teeth. In 1846, the American William Morton experimented with ether to anaesthetise his patients when having operations. The following year, Sir James Young Simpson of Edinburgh used chloroform to knock out a woman in childbirth. Queen Victoria was one of the first women to be anaesthetised.

The active substance in willow bark (salicylic acid) had been extracted during the 19th century. It was very bitter and harmed the stomach. Felix Hoffman was a chemist working for the German Bayer Company. His father had a lot of pain caused by arthritis. Hoffman experimented with the extract of willow and made a new drug. It was a lot more pleasant to use. Bayer started selling it in 1899 using the name 'aspirin'.

During the 20th century, chemists found many new substances that could ease pain including paracetamol and ibuprofen. Substances based on the extracts of opium are still very important. They are known as morphine, codeine and heroin. Scientists are also finding out the causes of pain and how the drugs work.

Questions

1 Which of the following painkillers is obtained from the opium poppy: codeine, aspirin, heroin, paracetamol, morphine?

2 Smoking opium and taking laudanum was a common habit in the 19th century. Why do you think that the British government (and others) made opium illegal early in the 20th century?

3 Acupuncture has become popular outside China. Why do many people use acupuncture instead of or in addition to painkillers and anaesthetics?

4 Why was the invention of the hypodermic syringe an important development?

5 Ether and chloroform have been replaced as anaesthetics. If too much was used the patient died. Despite the dangers, people were very keen to use ether or chloroform in surgery. Why was this?

6 Felix Hoffman tested his new painkiller on his father. What do you think his father felt about this?

7 Look at the painkillers you have in your home. Read the ingredients list. Which substance is the painkiller?

What makes plants grow?

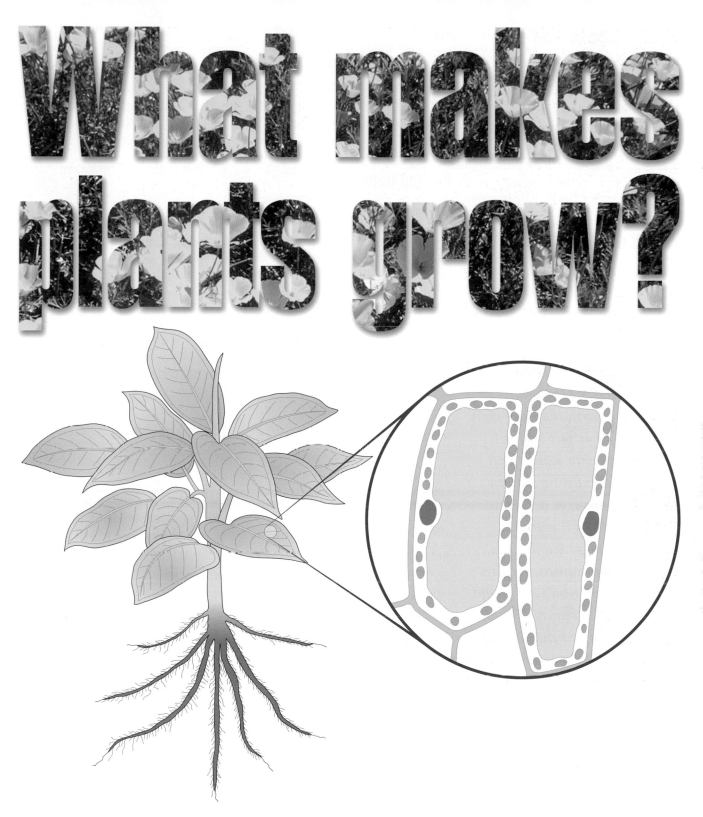

Students Fail science test

In a recent survey of American university students most couldn't answer simple science questions correctly. One question was about what makes plants grow. Most of the students thought that plants get all the nutrients they need from the soil.

Plant Food

If you are interested in gardening you will know all about plant foods. These are substances that you add to the soil to help plants grow. Usually one or two drops of liquid plant food are added to a litre of water. Is this all the food a plant needs to grow big and strong?

Plant a tree to save the planet

Burning fossil fuels is damaging the climate by increasing the amount of carbon dioxide in the atmosphere. Some people say that the answer is to plant trees. They say that trees 'soak up' carbon dioxide.

It's all water

What do plants need to make them grow? Do plants need 'food'?

Here is an experiment described by Jan Baptista van Helmont:

I took an Earthen vessel in which I put 200 pounds (91 kg) of Earth that had been dried in a Furnace which I moystened with Rainwater, and I implanted therein the Trunk or Stem, of a Willow Tree, weighing 5 pounds (2.3 kg); and at length, five years being finished, the Tree sprung from thence did weigh 169 pounds 3 ounces (77 kg). But I moystened the Earthen vessel with Rainwater ... and lest the dust should co-mingle with the Earth, I covered the lip or mouth of the Vessel, with an Iron Plate covered with Tin, and easily passable with many holes. At length, I again dried the Earth of the Vessel, and there were found the same 200 pound ... Therefore 164 pounds (74.7 kg) of Wood, Barks, and Roots arose out of water only ...

Van Helmont was a Belgian who lived from 1580–1644. It seems that his idea is not unlike those of the American students – plants use water to grow. At least van Helmont did an experiment and took some measurements.

Air and light

Almost a century after van Helmont, the Englishman Stephen Hales (1677–1761) did a similar experiment. He also planted a seedling but this time he enclosed the whole plant so that nothing could be lost or gained. Hales found that some of the air was used up. In other experiments he showed that plants only grow in the light. He also found that water passes through plants from the roots to the leaves and is lost by the process of transpiration. So although water is important to plants, thanks to Hale we know that the air is used as well and that plants need light.

Another leap forward in time brings us to the Austrian, Jan Ingen-Housz (1730–1799). By the time he died it was realised that there are different gases in the air. He performed experiments to show that plants can 'purify' the air when they are in light. This means that they make the air breathable again by releasing oxygen.

Little green bits

We now know that plants need water, air and light to grow, but where does it happen? During the 19th century microscopes improved a lot. The German, Julius von Sachs (1832–1897) looked at plant cells and found that they contained little green bits which he called chloroplasts. These contained the substance chlorophyll. Von Sachs showed that glucose was formed in the chloroplasts. Glucose is a carbohydrate that is turned into the starch and cellulose that make up most of a plant's mass.

Another German, Theodore Engelmann (1843–1909) took the story further. He placed the microscopic plant, spirogyra, under a source of light . He passed the light through a prism to split it up into the spectrum. Engelmann found that the chloroplasts absorbed red and blue light which is why they look green. It was the red and blue light that caused the glucose to be formed.

Photosynthesis

At last we can see where those American students went wrong. A plant takes in water through its roots and carbon dioxide from the air through its leaves. In light it builds carbohydrates. Plants do get other elements that they need from soil but these are in tiny amounts. About 40% of a plant is the element carbon which it gets from the air.

Solving the problem

After the Second World War, the American scientist Melvin Calvin used radioactive carbon-14 to follow what happens when a plant absorbs carbon dioxide. He made carbon dioxide containing the carbon-14 and blew it over a plant. At various times he took samples of the leaves and separated the substances in the cells. By measuring the radioactivity of the carbon-14 he was able to follow the carbon atoms through the

« Melvin Calvin, biochemist »

photosynthesis process. The different stages became known as the Calvin Cycle and he won the Nobel Prize in 1961.

Photosynthesis is a very complicated process. Scientists are still investigating how chlorophyll uses light energy to change carbon dioxide and water into sugars and oxygen. Other scientists are developing artificial photosynthesis. By using catalysts containing atoms of rare metals they can copy the reactions in leaves. Splitting water into hydrogen and oxygen is a vital part of photosynthesis. Scientists would like to be able to do this so that hydrogen can be made cheaply to use as a fuel. For now, plants are able to do the job much better than the scientists in their laboratories. ■

Questions

1 Find out more about the life and work of either van Helmont, Hales, Ingen-Housz, von Sachs, Engelmann or Calvin.

2 Why do you think many people believe that plants get all their nutrients from the soil?

3 a) In van Helmont's experiment, approximately how much water did the plant absorb (remember that most of a plant is carbohydrate which is approximately 40% carbon and 60% water)?

  b) Van Helmont probably gave the plant more water than this. What happened to the rest?

  c) Why did van Helmont find that the mass of the earth in the pot remained constant?

4 What did Hales do differently to van Helmont?

5 How did Engelmann's work explain why plants are green?

6 Melvin Calvin found that the leaves of a plant became radioactive after spending time in air containing carbon-14 dioxide. Explain this observation.

7 Why are scientists trying to make photosynthesis work artificially (i.e. without plants)?

Extra activities

1 Burning fossil fuels is increasing the amount of carbon dioxide in the air and causing the greenhouse effect. Since plants need carbon dioxide to grow, what will happen as the amount of the gas increases?

  a) The table below shows the result of an experiment in which maize was grown in two different samples of air.

Days	Leaf area (cm^2): 340 ppm CO_2	Leaf area (cm^2): 680 ppm CO_2
5	28	28
10	115	120
15	363	466
20	700	885
25	598	889

Source: http://www.arm.gov/docs/education/lessons/2act3.2.html

  Plot a graph of days (*x*-axis) against leaf area (*y*-axis) for the two sets of results.
  Describe the shape of the two graphs.
  What is the effect of increasing the amount of carbon dioxide?

  b) Some farmers grow crops in greenhouses with an increased amount of carbon dioxide in the air. What do the results suggest will be the effect of doing this?

  Other tests showed that plants grown in air containing a higher concentration of carbon dioxide contained less protein than normal. Why might this be a problem for farmers?

  c) Do you think that the increasing amount of carbon dioxide in the atmosphere will be harmful or of benefit?

What do plants want?

A little bit of this, a little bit of that

Take a plant, any plant will do, and burn it. Carbon dioxide and water vapour are given off and you are left with a grey ash. The ash contains many different elements – nitrogen, phosphorus, sulphur, calcium, magnesium, sodium, potassium, iron and tiny amounts of lots of other elements. Presumably the plant needs all these elements to grow properly, but where do they all come from?

Gone to waste

In the mid-19th century chemists, such as Justus von Liebig, began to realise that plants got most of the elements they needed from minerals in the soil. Liebig also realised that when crops were harvested and carried off to feed the growing population in cities, these nutrients were lost from the soil. On a visit to England he was appalled to find that sewage was wasted – it was being allowed to run into rivers and the sea. He suggested it should be put on farmland to replace the lost minerals.

The plant diet – bones, rock and a sprinkling of sulphuric acid

To keep his crops growing happily a farmer must supply them with the elements they need. But how do the plants like it? A lump of phosphorus here or a block of sodium there? Not likely! Like any discerning foodie, a plant likes its nutrients to come in just the right quantities and mixture.

Farmers found that crushed bones or bone-meal were a useful fertiliser and gave plants calcium and phosphorus. But sometimes the treatment didn't work.

In the 1830s, John Bennet Lawes had become interested in improving the crops on his estate at Rothamsted in Hertfordshire. His neighbours told him that sometimes bone-meal improved the harvest and sometimes it didn't. Lawes investigated and found that the bone-meal had to be treated with acid to make it soluble. Some soils were acidic and here the treatment worked, but in alkaline soils the bone-meal had no effect.

Lawes developed a process in which bone-meal or phosphate rock was treated with sulphuric acid. This produced a soluble fertiliser that he called superphosphate – it worked every time. In 1842, Lawes decided to start manufacturing and selling his fertiliser. His mother was appalled. Lawes was a gentleman and gentlemen did not involve themselves in 'trade'. Nevertheless, Lawes went into business and by the 1870s was making and selling 40 000 tonnes of superphosphate a year.

A gentlemen's disagreement

Do plants get their nitrogen from the soil too? This was a question that Lawes and his partner Henry Gilbert argued about with Liebig. Letters passed between Hertfordshire and Giessen, Germany and papers appeared in scientific publications.

Liebig said that the nitrogen came from the air. It dissolved in rainwater forming ammonia, which plants took in through their roots. He prepared a fertiliser for farmers to spread on fields that did not contain nitrogen.

Lawes and Gilbert disagreed. Their series of experiments at Rothamsted showed that unless manure or minerals containing nitrogen were added to the soil, crops would not grow successfully. They proved that Liebig's fertiliser alone was useless. On the other hand if ammonium nitrate or sodium nitrate or ammonium sulphate were added then crops would grow splendidly.

Eventually Liebig had to give in. Farmers realised that to keep their soil fertile they must add fertilisers containing nitrogen. It was a long time however before the details of the nitrogen cycle were worked out.

One hundred and sixty years, and counting

Henry Gilbert joined John Lawes at Rothamsted in 1843. Together they divided up the estate into lots of

> ## For thousands of years, millions of birds had flocked to the same beaches.

plots of land. In each plot they experimented to find out how different crops responded to different fertilisers. The experiments continued year after year.

In 1889, Lawes handed over the estate to a trust to continue the work and when he and Gilbert died just one year apart in 1900 their partnership had continued for nearly 60 years. But their work did not stop.

Today you can visit the Rothamsted Experimental Station and find some of Lawes's and Gilbert's experiments still going on, plus many others. Rothamsted is now part of the Institute of Arable Crop Research. As well as fertilisers and the growth of various crops, the Institute investigates pesticides and other aspects of agricultural research.

Full circle

Lawes's and Gilbert's conclusions led to some pretty strange trade. Farmers needed supplies of nitrogenous fertiliser. An excellent source was found on the beaches of Chile in South America. For thousands of years, millions of birds had flocked to the same beaches. Their droppings had built up into thick layers. In the late 19th century 200 000 tonnes a year of it

« **Rothamsted Laboratory where John Lawes's experiments continue** »

« Bird droppings on the beaches of Chile were a good source of nitrogen »

natural sources of nitrogen compounds – manure and sewage. At last Justus von Liebig is getting his way. ■

were being scraped off the beaches and transported to England.

Bird droppings are not an endless resource however and scientists looked for a way of converting nitrogen in the air into fertiliser. The German, Fritz Haber, was successful in the early years of the 20th century. For nearly 100 years the Haber process has provided farmers all over the world with the artificial fertiliser they need.

There are plenty of arguments against artificial fertilisers however. Organic farms insist on using

JUSTUS VON LIEBIG

« Justus von Liebig – famous German chemist »

Justus von Liebig was born in 1803 in Germany. His father sold drugs, dyes and other chemicals so it is not surprising that Liebig himself became interested in chemistry. As a young man he travelled to Paris to continue his studies. He was recommended for a professorship at the old university of Giessen when he was just 21years old. He stayed for 27 years before moving to Munich. He was one of the greatest chemists of the period and made many important discoveries. He also trained large numbers of students many of whom went on to become famous scientists themselves. He died in 1873.

JOHN BENNET LAWES

John Bennet Lawes was born in 1814. Lawes's father was a wealthy landowner in Hertfordshire but he died in 1822 leaving Lawes all his estates. He was educated at Eton and Oxford but became interested in science and set up his own laboratory at Rothamsted. In 1843, he was joined by Henry Gilbert and they spent the rest of their lives working on agricultural experiments. Lawes died in 1900.

« John Bennet Lawes – agricultural scientist »

The overflowing barrel

Plants need lots of different minerals in order to grow properly. Liebig illustrated the problem with this picture of a barrel. The barrel can only be filled with water up to the level of the lowest slat. This shows that a shortage of any element can limit the growth development of the plant.

The barrel slats are labelled: oxygen, light, water, warmth, carbon dioxide, soil conditions and other growth factors, chlorine, sulphur, iron, boron, manganese, zinc, copper, nitrogen, phosphorus, potassium, calcium, magnesium, molybdenum

Questions

1 Why do plants need nitrogen?

2 Why was bone-meal a successful fertiliser on acid soils but not on alkaline soils?

3 Why was Liebig upset by the way that the British got rid of their sewage?

4 Lawes in England and Liebig in Germany carried on their argument about fertilisers for many years. How did they communicate?

5 How was the argument between Lawes and Liebig settled?

6 Lawes's work at Rothamsted led to the development of the artificial fertiliser industry. It has been said that the growing population of the world has relied on processes such as the one invented by Fritz Haber to make ammonia. How important do you think artificial fertilisers have been? Why are many people against the use of artificial fertilisers today?

Extra activities

Lawes's and Gilbert's experiments at Rothamsted lasted many years, and are still going on. Plan an experiment to find out the effects of adding a fertiliser to the soil of a field in which a potato crop is grown each year.

DARWIN'S CRISIS

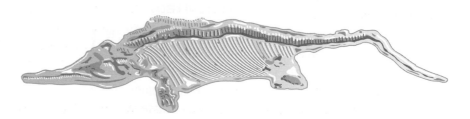

Charles Darwin is well known for his theory of evolution. What many people do not realise is how much he had to wrestle with his conscience before he could bring himself to publish his theory and how, ultimately, his work destroyed his Christian faith.

From Genesis to evolution

In late Georgian England, when Charles was growing up, things seemed simple. An eminent bishop had carefully calculated that God had created the human race at 9 o'clock in the morning on Sunday 23rd October 4004 BC. The full details could be found in the book of Genesis in the Old Testament of the Christian Bible. Further proof, if it was needed, was offered by William Paley. He saw evidence for a Divine Creator in the complexity of the human eye. 'How,' he argued, 'could something so perfect have come about except as the work of an intelligent Creator?'

Then things started to go wrong. Mary Anning had started a lucrative trade in dinosaur fossils she found near her home in Lyme Regis. These creatures had obviously existed and died out. And they certainly hadn't been mentioned in the creation story.

« Mary Anning's trade in dinosaur fossils made some people ask questions about where they fitted into the Genesis story of creation »

Jean-Baptiste Lamarck suggested that animals could develop new characteristics that helped them to survive. The giraffe, he argued, had developed a long neck to help it reach the tops of trees. Animals that did not develop into useful species would be the ones that died out. Yet according to William Paley, if God had created all things, they should be perfect and not need to develop new characteristics. Although he didn't know it (and his theory was wrong!), Lamarck was paving the way for the theory of evolution.

Charles Darwin was keen on natural history – it was a very fashionable hobby for well-to-do young men at the time. But he was, like almost everyone else in Britain at the time, a practising Christian and he was thinking about a career as a clergyman. However life has a way of turning things on its head. Charles was offered the chance to sail round South America on the *HMS Beagle* as the ship's naturalist. 'An ideal way to spend a gap year,' he thought, and went.

Five years later, having made pages and pages of notes of what he saw, he returned and tried to make sense of it all. His evidence certainly didn't seem to point to a divine creator, or even to a specific creation event.

'Why,' he thought, 'would God have gone to the trouble of creating several species like ostriches in Africa, emus in Australia and rheas in South America, when one would do?' What ever he looked at, plants and animals, he saw evidence of change and adaptation. But how could that happen?

« Lamarck thought that creatures developed characteristics that helped them survive. He was wrong, but his ideas started people thinking »

Thomas Malthus had an idea. Malthus had worked out that there was competition in nature and that the fittest survived. And, when Darwin read this, it proved to be the missing link he needed for his theory.

Charles had taken over 20 years to work out his theory. All the time he was trying to reconcile his science with his Christian faith. He was also concerned not to upset his wife, who was a devout Christian. He might have put his findings aside for much longer if it hadn't been for Alfred Wallace.

Alfred had come up with a similar theory. If Charles didn't publish his theory now, Alfred would get the credit. But if Charles did publish he might be a laughing stock and be discredited as a scientist. It was a

« 'Why did God go to the trouble of creating three types when one would do?' thought Darwin »

« Darwin's theory is well-established, yet some people still teach the creation story as if it is also an acceptable theory »

terrible decision to make. In the end the two men got together and agreed to present their ideas together – there's safety in numbers!

The theory was outrageous, for its time. The Bishop of Oxford tried to prove it was wrong, poking fun at Darwin by asking whether he really believed his grandfather was an ape. Others were more open-minded and, after looking at the evidence, supported the controversial ideas.

Alfred Wallace continued to collect evidence for evolution and supported Darwin's efforts to get the theory of evolution accepted. He earned his living from writing and lecturing about his expeditions. The British Government gave him a pension in 1880 and he lived until 1913.

In the end, Darwin's fame and reputation as a scientist were made, and the rest, as they say, is history! Or is it?

Even though Darwin's theory of evolution is accepted as a well-established explanation for the diversity of species, there are people who still prefer the simple description offered in the Bible. There are states in the USA where both the theory of evolution and the Bible story of Genesis are taught as equally correct. Some parents even withdraw their children from lessons where the theory of evolution is discussed and insist that the Biblical version is the one they should be taught. ■

Questions

1 Why did Darwin have to wrestle with his conscience before he could publish his theory of evolution?

2 What evidence did people put forward for the creation story as the correct description of how people came to exist?

3 What evidence did Darwin put forward for his theory of evolution?

4 Other scientists influenced Darwin as he perfected his theory. Who were these scientists and what were their ideas?

5 What finally prompted Darwin to publish his theory?

Discussion

What is your opinion on what should be taught in schools on this subject? Should both the theory of evolution and the creation story be taught alongside each other to allow people to make up their own minds? Explain your position.

Extra activities

Look at the website of the National Center for Science Education in America http://www.natcenscied.org to read about legal cases against teachers who teach the theory of evolution.

Mendel's peas

Prince Harry, the son of Charles, the Prince of Wales, and Diana, Princess of Wales, has auburn hair. Prince Charles has brown hair and Diana was blond.

Charles Darwin would have been completely confused by this. He was convinced that the characteristics of the parents blended together to create their offsprings' characteristics. He had a very large family so we can only conclude that his children all resembled their two parents equally.

Gregor Mendel never had children and we don't know what colour his hair was. But he could have explained the unexpected appearance of red hair in children of brown or blond haired parents.

Although he was working at the same time as Darwin, Mendel's ideas never made it as far as England. In fact they were ignored for the whole of Mendel's life. This was partly because he only published them in a very obscure

« Red hair is a characteristic that can miss a generation. Mendel explained how »

« These scientists worked at the same time but never heard about each other's work. They would have made much greater progress if they had! »

Mendel's experiment

Mendel took peas with different characteristics – long stems and short stems, red flowers and white flowers, smooth seeds and knobbly seeds. He took pollen from one plant and placed it carefully in the stigma of another. Then he waited. When the new plant appeared he recorded accurately what characteristics it had. For example, he

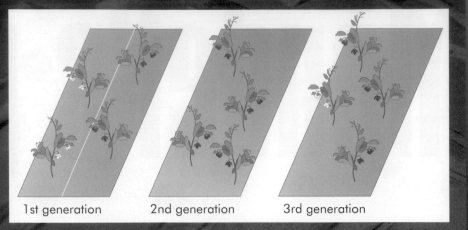

1st generation   2nd generation   3rd generation

《 Mendel's work showed that a characteristic does not just disappear. It can reappear in the next generation 》

bred red-flowered plants with white-flowered plants. The new plants all had red flowers. This might lead you to think that the red characteristic has wiped out the white (a bit like one red sock turning all the white socks red in the washing machine!). But then Mendel went on to breed these red plants with each other. What he didn't get was another set of red plants! Instead one in four of the plants had white flowers!

He worked out that if a plant had the factor for a red flower, you got a red flower – but the plant might also have a factor for a white flower which it could still pass on to its offspring. If an offspring got a white plant factor from both parents (even if they had red flowers) it could then be white!

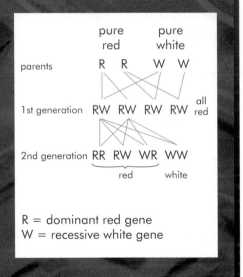

R = dominant red gene
W = recessive white gene

journal and partly because everyone who read them didn't really understand the significance of what Mendel had done.

Mendel was a monk. In the early 19th century, in what is now the Czech Republic, entering a monastery was the only way for a poor boy to get a good education. The abbot of the monastery supported Mendel's request to study science but put his foot down when Mendel suggested he bred mice. The abbot considered it inappropriate for a monk to be

studying the sex-lives of animals!

Instead Mendel studied the sex lives of peas. He continually cross-bred peas and made careful results tables of the flower colour produced by certain combinations of pea plant. After he had collected over 20 000 results he felt confident that he understood what was going on.

Mendel suggested the idea of 'factors', which carried each characteristic. We now call these 'factors' genes. Mendel went on to

explain how these factors were passed on from parent to offspring. He could even explain how a characteristic can be absent from a parent and then turn up in the offspring – exactly as red hair does.

Although Mendel published his results in 1866 his ideas remained hidden until 1900. The other monks had burned all his papers when he died, but the obscure journal where his paper was published was still in a library in Holland. Hugo de Vries happened to read the journal and suddenly he realised how important Mendel's work was.

Once it was out in the open, Mendel's work was repeated and his results checked. If Darwin had read it he would have been delighted to see how Mendel's ideas fitted into his own theory of evolution. But Darwin died in 1882.

By the 1950s, the idea of genes was well established. James Watson, Francis Crick and Rosalind Franklin got as far as working out that DNA resembled a spiral staircase. Mendel's factors were now called genes and the scientists had worked out that the genes were strips of the DNA every living thing has in every cell of its body.

By the 1990s, genetic modification was in the news. Scientists could take tiny parts of the DNA from the cell of one living thing and insert it into the cell of another. This way they could transfer characteristics immediately between living things.

The benefits and problems associated with this are controversial. Genetic modification can help to cure fatal diseases and can allow crops to be grown more efficiently. But people are concerned that there are dangers associated with changing the genetic code of people and of plants. They argue that we cannot be sure that illness will not emerge in the future as a result of these experiments. ■

« **Crick and Watson got the Nobel Prize for their work on DNA. Franklin missed out because she died before the prize was awarded** »

Questions

1 Why would Charles Darwin have found it very difficult to explain how a child with red hair can be born to parents with brown of blond hair?

2 Mendel did lots of experiments to find out how characteristics were passed on from one generation to the next. Explain Mendel's idea of how this worked. Draw a diagram to help your explanation.

3 Darwin never heard about Mendel's work even though he lived at about the same time. Why was this?

4 How did Mendel's results become well known?

5 Scientists are always trying to get their work published in journals but it's not just a matter of sending the paper in. The work has to be refereed by other scientists. This means that other scientists who do similar work read and think about the experiment and decide whether they think the results make sense. Only if they are convinced, will the journal publish the paper. Why do the journals insist that papers are refereed this way?

6 Why are scientists always keen to read about the work of other scientists in journals and try the experiments for themselves?

Extra activities

Genetic modification is a topic often written about in newspapers. Find out about genetic modification. Then look at some newspaper reports to see if you think it is correctly reported.

Improving humans

Is the human race still evolving? Some people say that natural selection no longer kills off the weak, the handicapped or the foolish. In developed countries that may be true. One hundred years ago Francis Galton and his followers wanted to encourage human evolution. They wanted humans to improve physically and mentally in order to have a happier life. Galton founded the science of eugenics to measure and control human inheritance. Since the Second World War, eugenics has become a science that few scientists admit to studying.

Who was Francis Galton and what is eugenics?

THE TRAVELLER

Francis Galton had a very happy childhood. He was the youngest child of a wealthy family in Birmingham. His mother's father was Erasmus Darwin and so he was a cousin of Charles Darwin. He was a very bright youngster and his parents intended that he should study medicine. In 1840, at the age of 18 and following some training in Birmingham and London, he went to Cambridge University to study medicine. In fact he spent most of his time studying maths and then had a nervous breakdown. He left university without his degree.

In 1844, Galton's father died leaving him very wealthy indeed. Now he was free to do what he liked. He set off for Egypt and on his return tried to live the life of a country gentleman. But the travel-bug had got into him and in 1850 he embarked for South West Africa. After two years travelling and writing he returned to England. The Royal Geographical Society awarded him a gold medal for his account of the geography of the area.

« Francis Galton »

He married Louisa Butler and became a gentleman of science. Galton became interested in meteorology and over the next ten years became respected for his collection of weather data and skill at noticing weather patterns.

GALTON AND EVOLUTION

With his knowledge of mathematics and his experience of meeting people from different parts of the world, Francis Galton began to think about the characteristics which were passed from one generation to another. When Charles Darwin's book, *The Origin of the Species*, was published in 1859 he became very interested in evolution and natural selection. For him it seemed that human civilisation was trying to avoid the effects of natural selection by feeding the weak and treating the sick. He was convinced that individuals with high intelligence and good physical characteristics were overwhelmed by society and that their qualities became lost in succeeding generations.

Like Darwin, Galton wondered how hereditary characteristics were passed from parents to children. He thought that genetic material was carried in the blood. He carried out experiments where he passed blood from one rabbit to another. After a few rabbit generations he had to admit that his blood transfusions had no effect.

In the 1860s, Galton began investigating the qualities of British families. He concluded that desirable characteristics such as intelligence and physical fitness declined over the generations to an average value. He published his first paper in 1865 in which he classified the British population into 16 classes of intelligence.

THE SCIENCE OF EUGENICS

To develop his ideas further, Galton needed more data on British people. In the 1880s he invented the lottery questionnaire. A booklet of questions was sent to hundreds of families to fill in. He offered a chance to win £500 of prizes to encourage people to complete and return the booklets to him. The

responses contributed to his study of a new science, which he called 'eugenics'.

The aim of eugenics was to determine the hereditary characteristics that Galton thought would improve the happiness of humans. To do this would mean interfering with the natural mating habits of people. Galton realised that it would require public support in order to 'check the birth-rate of the unfit' and to achieve 'the improvement of the race by furthering the productivity of the fit'.

« **Poor children suffered from rickets** »

For Galton, the 'unfit' included the diseased and the criminals. He suggested that children with rickets, a crippling disease that caused the bones to be weak and bent, should not be allowed to have children themselves. He did not know that rickets was caused simply by a lack of vitamin D.

AFTER GALTON

Francis Galton received a lot of support for his ideas. Many educated and prosperous people saw it as their duty to improve the physical and intellectual qualities of the human race. Galton contributed to the establishment of an eugenics research group at University College London. When he died in 1911 his will provided for a Professor of Eugenics at the University.

During the 1920s and 1930s the Eugenics movement grew in Britain, the USA and elsewhere and influenced the policies of governments. The science found its biggest support in Germany under the Nazis. Nazi policies to purify and improve the German race lead to the murder of 6 million Jews and many thousands of 'degenerates' such as gypsies, homosexuals and the mentally handicapped.

The horrors that were discovered after the fall of the Nazis in 1945 turned people away from eugenics and Galton's hopes for improving the human race. The science became associated with racism, fascism and intolerance of minorities.

Eugenics and genetics

Many of Francis Galton's theories and classifications of peoples have been discredited but the modern science of genetics offers a new form of eugenics. Genetic testing of parents and their embryos can detect undesirable characteristics. We may see nothing unethical in choosing a baby free of diseases such as cystic fibrosis, but the technology of genetic engineering has further possibilities. It may become possible to choose the genome of babies to make sure that they are intelligent, handsome and athletic. Alternatively, some parents may choose to have a disabled child. The case of deaf parents deciding to have a child who is deaf has already happened.

If the cloning of human embryos becomes possible, then there is the temptation to clone only those babies that have the most desired characteristics. We may attempt to produce Francis Galton's improved human race.

The question that troubled Galton and many others is this – what has the most effect on the intelligence of a child? Is it their inherited characteristics (nature) or the environment in which they grow up (nuture)? Francis Galton was convinced that inheritance played the major part. The advances in genetics at first suggested that Galton was correct. There seemed to be genes for every physical characteristic, so perhaps intelligence was also governed by genes. Later discoveries about how the genes affect the way the brain develops have suggested that intellectual development depends on other factors such as diet during infancy. The question of whether genes or upbringing have the biggest influence on intelligence still cannot be answered.

FRANCIS GALTON AND FINGERPRINTS

A problem for police and courts in the late 19th century was identifying people suspected of committing crimes. How were they to know that people were who they said they were? Various ideas had been tried out but fingerprints turned out to be the most reliable one.

« Galton's book about fingerprinting »

Francis Galton had looked at fingerprints as a way of identifying a person's race or heredity. After examining the fingerprints of hundreds of people he finally decided that they had nothing to do with race or family background. But he did notice that every person's fingerprints were unique and that they did not change over the years. Galton worked out a way of classifying the arches and whorls and special points, which made one set of fingerprints different from another. He calculated that there was a 1 in 64 billion chance of two people having the same fingerprint classification. Galton's method is still very much the method used by police across the world today.

CYRIL BURT AND IQ TESTING

Francis Galton tried to find links between intelligence and inherited characteristics, such as height. He failed but the idea that intelligence was hereditary was central to Cyril Burt's work on IQ (intelligence quotient). Burt was born in 1883 and become Professor of Psychology at University College London. In the 1920s he developed intelligence tests with which he tested pairs of identical twins. His results showed a strong link between intelligence, or IQ, and ethnic and family background. Burt's findings were used in the late 1940s to develop the 11+ examination, which selected children for grammar schools.

It was only after his death in 1971 that it was found that Burt had falsified many of his results and exaggerated the inherited aspect of intelligence. What is more, his IQ tests were biased against people who came from other places and had little experience of British society and culture. Burt's work was discredited and once again the nature or nurture debate was opened up.

Questions

1 Why did Francis Galton do experiments to transfuse blood between rabbits?

2 Francis Galton's classification of British families showed that poor families often had low intellectual abilities. What explanations can you give for this?

3 Why do you think that Galton's eugenics became popular early in the 20th century?

4 Why has eugenics come to be considered 'bad' or 'unethical' science?

Discussion

1 What physical characteristics have you inherited from each of your parents?
   Can you think of any mental characteristics that you share with your parents? (For example, do you and one of your parents have a talent for mathematics, art, music, or do you have similar aspects to your characters, like telling jokes or having a temper etc.)
   If you have a talent, do you think you inherited it or have your parents just encouraged it?

2 Imagine you are a poor person who has often been ill. If Galton's eugenic plans had been in force you would have been told not to have children so that the human race could be improved. How would you respond? Would you be content not to have children if it meant that the human race could evolve?

3 In the future it is proposed that genetic testing and engineering could be used to choose the characteristics of babies? Should parents or governments have this right? Discuss the arguments for and against this proposal?

Extra activities

Look at your fingerprints. What shapes are they? If you have an inkpad, take prints of some of the pupils in your class. Mix the prints up then see if you can match the print to their fingers.

Scientists have studied anatomy at Oxford since the 17th century. The Department of Human Anatomy at Oxford University was formed over 100 years ago. When Professor Kay Davies was appointed as the head of the department in 1998 the title changed to Human Anatomy and Genetics. Kay is looking for the cause and remedies for diseases in which people lose their muscles.

People with muscular dystrophy do not have the gene that produces a particular protein. The protein protects the membrane in muscles. It would be impossible to replace the gene in every muscle. Kay has found another gene that produces a similar protein. This gene is not normally active in adult muscle. Kay's team is looking for substances that could switch on this gene and prevent the loss of muscles.

Kay's team is also working on the gene that is responsible for another disease, spinal muscular atrophy. They are looking at how this gene works in the muscle cells in a worm and a fly. They hope to get ideas about what the gene actually does in humans.

An interview with
Professor Kay Davies

PE: What made you decide to follow a scientific career?

KD: I was very good at maths and chemistry at school and was inspired by my chemistry teacher who persuaded me that chemistry was the secret of biological function. I then decided to do chemistry at Oxford. I have always wanted to do medical research even as a ten-year-old.

PE: Where have you studied and worked?

KD: I did my undergraduate and graduate studies in Oxford. After a two-year postdoctoral fellowship in Oxford I worked in a laboratory just outside Paris (France) for two years. I returned to work in London for three years at St Mary's Hospital in Paddington. I then moved back to Oxford to continue working on muscular dystrophy at the John Radcliffe Hospital. In 1995, I moved my laboratory to the central university science site where I took up the Chair of Genetics.

PE: What has given you the greatest pleasure as a scientist?

KD: Working with the families suffering from neuromuscular disease and interacting with many scientists worldwide. We have collaborations in the US, the Netherlands, Belgium, Italy, Australia and France.

PE: Which scientist (past or present) do you admire most?

KD: Dorothy Hodgkin. She did brilliant work, fought for what she thought was right for the world and fitted in having a family!

PE: What benefit do you think your research will have for the next generation?

KD: My research and the approaches we now use will have an impact on the treatment of many genetic diseases in the future.

PE: Did you experience any difficulties because you are a female scientist?

KD: Yes, but the situation is getting better. The higher you get the more difficult it gets and there are so few other women with top academic posts. It should improve with the next generation.

PE: What do you do to relax?

KD: I go to the gym, read, listen to music or go walking.

PE: What other career might you have liked to follow?

KD: I was always very good at maths but I had no other ambition except medical science of some sort.

PE: Where and when was your favourite holiday?

KD: The barrier reef in Australia thirteen years ago. The scenery is so beautiful and the area is relatively unspoilt.

PE: What is your favourite food?

KD: Fish.

PE: What do you consider to be the biggest threat and opportunity for mankind in the future?

KD: The biggest threat is terrorism which threatens people's security and freedom.
   The opportunity is to use all the new technology to increase communication and food supplies around the whole world.

PE: What piece of modern technology could you not do without?

KD: A microwave oven.

PE: Thank you, Professor Davies.

First published in *Breakthrough*, **1**, no.1, Jan. 99

DOROTHY CROWFOOT HODGKIN

(1910–1994) was among the first women to study chemistry at Oxford University. She then spent a short time at Cambridge University where she learnt how to use X-rays to study the structure of molecules. She returned to Oxford to set up an X-ray department and stayed

« Dorothy Hodgkin – Nobel Prize-winning chemist »

there for the rest of her career. She found the structure of penicillin and the vitamin B_{12}. After over 30 years' work she completed the structure of insulin. She was awarded the Nobel Prize for Chemistry in 1964 and is the only British woman to win the prize. She married and had three children. She was a pacifist and very active in politics.

Questions

1 Professor Davies has investigated the muscles of a worm. What is her reason for doing this?

2 Professor Davies says that she enjoys collaborating with scientists in other countries. How do scientists keep in touch with each other's work?

Extra activities

1 Find out about the effects of muscular dystrophy.

2 Get in touch with some more scientists and find out what their work and life is like.

@ WEBSITES @

http://www.anat.ox.ac.uk

Meet the ancestors

Out of Africa

The human population of the Earth is 6 billion and rising. Despite our different shapes, sizes and colours, we can all interbreed and so we are all one species. This means that according to Darwin's theory of evolution we are all descended from one family.

Scientists think that a family of apes somewhere in Africa was the ancestors of the human race. A mutation in the DNA of one member of this family produced variations that set the family apart from other apes. The family of apes probably faced life-threatening situations but they survived, perhaps because the mutations had given them some special advantages. Eventually their numbers grew and they became a clan. Members of the clan travelled from their homeland, eventually settling in every part of the world except Antarctica.

When did all this happen? Well, that is where the arguments start.

All about Eve

Have you ever owned a pet hamster? Hamsters come in all

« The human race seems to be made up of many different ethnic groups »

sorts of colours and sizes, short-haired and long-haired, but did you know that every single pet hamster across the whole world is descended from one female discovered in 1930?

The same is true of the human race except that it is a bit longer since our ancestral mother lived. Allan Wilson of the University of California at Berkeley, USA looked at the mitochondrial DNA of 147 people who were randomly selected. The similarities in their DNA suggested that they were all related and descended from one woman. DNA picks up mutations

over a long period of time and acts a bit like a clock. From the number of variations between the DNA of his subjects, Wilson worked out that the ancestral mother lived about 200 000 years ago. Perhaps it wasn't surprising that this long dead woman became known as Eve from the story in the Bible.

Other scientists did not agree with Allan Wilson's results. Milford Wolpoff of the University of Michigan said that it was at least a million years ago that humans had developed from a single female. He said that fossils showed that creatures resembling humans, but

« **All of the human race is descended from the children of one woman** »

not quite the same as us, had spread across the world. Wolpoff suggested that these creatures had evolved to become the humans that we are today.

A little later, two of Allan Wilson's colleagues, Linda Vigilant and Mark Stoneking repeated Wilson's experiment, using 189 people including 121 from Africa. They came up with the same result. We are all descended from one woman living 200 000 years ago.

The arguments continue about when humans spread out of Africa but there seems little doubt that we are all the children of Eve.

What became of Eve's children and when did they arrive in Europe? Archaeologists have argued for a long time about when the various tribes and clans moved across Europe and when agriculture replaced hunting and gathering.

Bryan Sykes, the professor of Human Genetics at Oxford University became interested in the problem. He has spent his career investigating the DNA of people with genetic diseases. Professor Sykes found various genes that could decide whether people would fall ill in the future. Then he decided to look back into the past. Like Allan Wilson he looked at the mitochondrial DNA, but Professor Sykes chose a large number of European people. He found that people mainly belonged to just

seven clans each with an ancestral mother. These seven women had lived in different parts of Europe at various times up to 50 000 years ago. These women were the 'Seven Daughters of Eve' that Sykes writes about in his book.

Many people like to know their ancestry and so Professor Sykes

« **Dryan Sykes, author of *The Seven Daughters of Eve* »**

Thanks Mum!

Mitochondria are tiny objects found in nearly all cells. They manage the energy production for the cell. They have their own small ribbons of DNA, which carry the genes for respiration. The egg cells produced by women have mitochondria but sperm do not. When an egg is fertilised and becomes an embryo all the mitochondria come from the egg cell, which carry the mother's DNA. Every one of us has the mitochondrial DNA of our mothers, which she got from her mother, and her mother …

« **Mitochondria provide the energy for cells and have their own DNA** » has formed a company, Oxford Ancestors, that can tell you which one of the seven women is your great, thousand times great, grandmother. All you need do is scrape some cheek cells into an envelope and send it with the fee to Oxford Ancestors.

Home is where your genes come from

We may all be descended from one woman but in western society we have traditionally taken our names from our fathers. Many people are interested in geneology and wish to find out who their ancestors were and where they came from. Professor Bryan Sykes wondered if all the Sykes' were related. He plotted a map of Great Britain and found that many Sykes lived around the Yorkshire town of Huddersfield. This wasn't too surprising as the name Sykes comes from a word for a moorland stream, used in the Yorkshire Dales. Professor Sykes contacted a large number of men with his surname and asked for a sample of cheek cells from each. From the replies he got he was able to show that over half had very similar genes on the Y chromosome. Sykes was able to calculate that the DNA was so similar that there could only be one man from whom they were descended who lived about 700 years ago. Professor Sykes traced the ancestral father to the village of Flockton on the moors near Huddersfield.

What about the Sykes who didn't have the same DNA? Well of course some people change their name, perhaps adopting the name of a stepfather. Another reason is that throughout history women

Thanks Dad!

Women have two X chromosomes but men have an X and a Y chromosome. It is the Y chromosome that makes a baby become a male. The sperms produced by a man either contain a copy of his X chromosome or of his Y chromosome. If it is the Y carrying sperm that fertilises an egg the child will be male and carry his father's Y chromosome. He in turn will pass on the Y chromosome to his male children. Over the generations the Y chromosome, like all the chromosomes, picks up mutations. Only identical twins will definitely have exactly the same DNA. Nevertheless there are enough similarities between son and father and grandfather and so on back through the generations, to be able to detect the family link.

have occasionally had children fathered by men who were not their husbands. Professor Sykes has calculated that in fact the Sykes' wives have been relatively faithful with only a small proportion of children being born with the wrong fathers.

Professor Sykes has worked back to the ancestral fathers of a number of family names. You too can have your family history worked out for a fee. ■

References

Lewin, R. (1991) DNA evidence strengthens Eve hypothesis, *New Scientist*, **132**, no. 1791, Oct.

Wolpoff, M. & Thorne, A. (1991) The Case against Eve, *New Scientist*, **130**, no. 1774, June.

Questions

1 What feelings do you have about knowing that if you are a European you are descended from one of just seven women and that we are all descended from one African woman?

2 Is there any useful purpose to finding to whom you are related?

3 Allan Wilson was a geneticist while Milford Wolpoff was a palaeontologist working with human fossils. Why did they disagree over the origins of humans? Why do most people now accept Wilson's theory of an ancestral mother of the human race?

Extra activities

Draw up your family tree. Show on it your parents, grandparents and any brothers, sisters, aunts, uncles and cousins. Mark on it the women who have given you your mitochondrial DNA. Also mark on the family tree the other relatives who will have the same female ancestors as you.

If you are a boy, mark on your family tree the men who gave you your Y chromosome and the other males who share it with you. If you are a girl, trace the ancestors of your father who share the Y chromosome.

The case of the salty sweat

David is 29 years old. He is quite short and thin. He's coughing. He coughs a lot. David finds breathing difficult, but at least it is time for his massage. The physiotherapist thumps his chest and back with her cupped hand. David coughs again and spits out thick sticky mucus. His chest feels lighter and he can breathe more easily – for now.

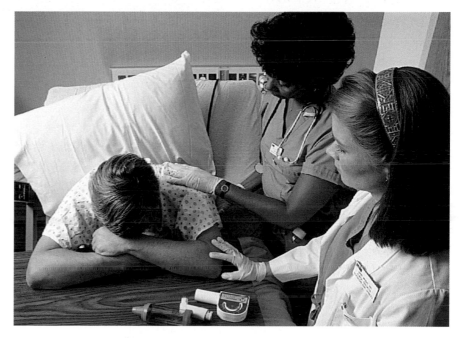

Finding the problem

Soon after he was born, David's mother noticed that he wasn't well. David wasn't putting on weight. He had trouble breathing. David's mother also noticed that when she kissed him his skin tasted salty. It didn't take the doctor long to solve the mystery. David had cystic fibrosis or CF.

David can tell you about his childhood:

I was away from school a lot. I caught colds all the time. It was always difficult to breathe, but colds made it worse. I was eating a lot too. The problem is most of the food I eat goes straight through me and makes my poo look strange. I have to have a special diet with extra carbohydrates and proteins. The doctors said I must play sport. I like swimming and football, but I get tired quickly and I start coughing.

As I got older, things got worse. Some days I needed hours and hours of massage to get the mucus out of my lungs. I'm getting some new medicine now so I'm feeling better. I'm looking forward to my 30th birthday. Many CF sufferers don't last this long.

David's doctor explains his problems:

Cystic fibrosis or CF is a genetic disease. A gene controls the amount of salt in cells. Everyone has two copies of the gene. We get one copy from our mother and one from our father. In CF sufferers like David, both copies are faulty. The faulty genes affect the lungs and the pancreas the most. In the lungs a thick mucus is formed which blocks up the airways. It traps germs, so David gets lots of infections. In the pancreas the CF gene stops enzymes getting to the intestines. This means that David doesn't digest all his food.

Treating the disease with genes

Not long ago babies with CF died after a few months. Today the treatment is better. In the future scientists hope to cure CF. The solution is gene therapy. David explains what this means:

The gene that causes all my problems is a little bit of DNA, which is in all my cells. If the DNA could be changed then I would be cured. That is what gene therapy does. Sounds simple doesn't it? Unfortunately it is more difficult than that. It is impossible to change the DNA in all the cells in my body. Scientists have tried to change the DNA in the cells of my airways. They're the cells that produce the mucus that causes most of my problems.

Even altering these cells isn't easy. Somehow the correct bit of DNA has to replace the faulty bit. Scientists have taken the piece of DNA out of cells from healthy people. Then they've put the DNA inside a virus. Actually they use a cold virus. I'm always catching colds so that is a good idea. The virus is mixed into a spray.

Every day I squirt the spray down my throat. The viruses attack the cells on the surface of my airways – just like cold viruses do. The virus puts the new bit of DNA into my cells. The cells work properly and do not make as much mucus. I feel a lot better.

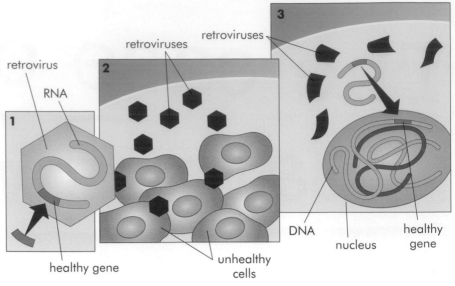

retrovirus

RNA

retroviruses

retroviruses

DNA

nucleus

healthy gene

healthy gene

unhealthy cells

Gene therapy is not a total cure as David says.

Unfortunately the effects of the spray don't last. The cells that have been changed don't live for very long. The cells that replace them have got my wrong version of the gene. I'm back to wheezing and coughing. At least I've improved a little.

Scientists are looking at better ways of getting the correct gene into David's cells.

All in the family

David knows that there is not much chance that he'll be cured of CF. He is worried that if he or his sister Megan had children they might have the disease. Megan describes the problem:

I was five years old when David was born. I was fit and healthy. I remember how worried my parents were when they found out that David had CF. I didn't have it so I wasn't bothered until I grew up.

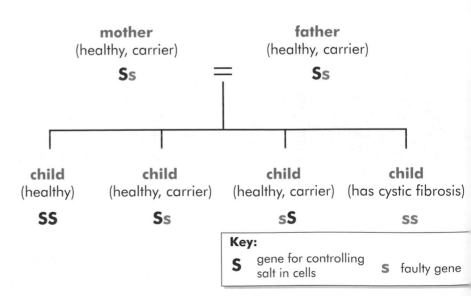

mother
(healthy, carrier)
Ss

father
(healthy, carrier)
Ss

child
(healthy)
SS

child
(healthy, carrier)
Ss

child
(healthy, carrier)
sS

child
(has cystic fibrosis)
ss

Key:
S gene for controlling salt in cells

s faulty gene

When I was going out with my boyfriend, Paul, I started to think about having a baby myself. Would my children have CF?

Paul explains what they did:

We knew that Megan's parents must each have one faulty CF gene in their cells. When they had children, one in four had a chance of getting the disease. That was David's bad luck. But two in four would carry one copy of the bad gene. They wouldn't get ill but could pass it on to their own children. We had to find out if Megan was a carrier.

Megan continues the story:

The doctor took some cells from inside my cheek and sent them away to be tested. We were told that they can separate out the DNA from my cells. Then they check to see which version of the CF gene I've got. It turned out that both my genes are correct. Only one in four of my parent's children would be like me, so I've been lucky. Paul was tested too. There's no CF in his family, so it was just to make certain that he is not a carrier. He wasn't, so now we know that all our children will be free of CF. ■

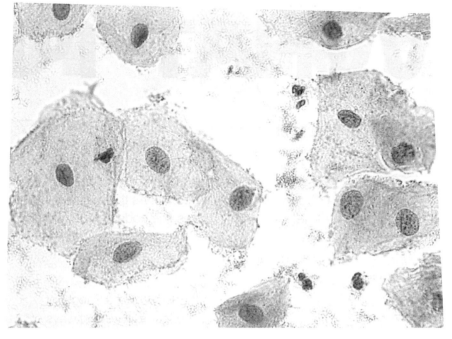

《 **The nucleus shows up clearly in this stained cell. The DNA is contained in the nucleus** 》

Questions

1 Babies often have coughs and colds. What bit of evidence made David's doctor think that he might have CF?

2 All the cells in David's body contain the CF gene but it is only switched on in some organs. Which organs are affected most?

3 CF and other genetic diseases are caused by a gene not working, as it should. How does gene therapy provide a cure?

4 David's sister, Megan, was fit. Why was she concerned about any children she might have in the future?

5 Explain why only one in four children of some parents get the disease while two out of four may be a carrier.

In the UK, every week five babies are born with cystic fibrosis. One person in every 25 is a carrier of the faulty gene.

Extra activities

When Megan becomes pregnant, doctors could test the genes of the fetus very early in the pregnancy. Some people think that this type of genetic testing is wrong. Parents may decide to abort a baby if it has a genetic disease. Parents may even choose to have babies that have the genes for beauty, or intelligence or sporting ability, if they exist. Discuss whether you think genetic testing of babies is a good thing and in what cases it should be used.

@ WEBSITES @

http://www.cftrust.org.uk

arrangement of bases in each gene? What does each gene do? These are called 'rationalistic' questions. The story of the race between the HGP and Celera raises other questions. How should the research be organised? Who should pay? What do we do with the information? These are the kinds of questions we face in all aspects of our daily lives. They are called 'naturalistic' questions. Scientists are faced with both types of question and have to find answers for them all, but the rest of us also need to think about answers to the 'naturalistic' questions of science. ■

What the HGP may do for us

- **More scientific knowledge:** Knowing more about the human genome adds to the store of what is known about the natural world (which includes us).
- **New scientific techniques:** Development and discovery of more efficient ways of sequencing DNA base pairs can benefit other areas of science and technology.
- **International co-operation and communication:** The HGP is too large for one country to undertake on its own. Therefore the HGP is an international project.
- **Isolation of the alleles ('type of gene') causing various genetic diseases:** Knowing a great deal more about the causes of such diseases increases the possibility that treatments, and even cures, can be found.
- **Find more clues to 'human nature':** Understanding more about the genetic code for humans could increase knowledge about what it means to be 'human'.

What problems the HGP may bring us

- **Expense:** At the start of the project the cost of 'sequencing' one DNA 'base' did cost US $1.00. The aim was to reduce the cost to US $0.01 per base. However it soon rose to US $2.00. The money comes out of taxpayers' pockets.
- **Invasion of privacy:** People who have their DNA sequenced do not have control over how the information is used. The Institution that took the sample can use the knowledge it gains for its own purposes. The question that is being asked is: 'Is this ethical?'
- **Using the knowledge ethically:** If the knowledge becomes available to everyone, then some scientists could use the information in unethical ways. For instance, the DNA of human embryos fertilised in a laboratory could be sequenced. Only those embryos with characteristics that the parents (or other interested parties) desired would be implanted in the mother's womb. Such characteristics could include the sex of the embryo, its external appearance when it became a child, its intelligence, its sporting ability, etc. The remaining embryos with 'undesirable' characteristics would not be used.

Questions

1 Explain what you understand by the term 'genome'.

2 Why was it expected that the Human Genome Project would be more expensive and require more work than John Sulston's work on the genome of the nematode worm?

3 What was surprising about the human genome?

4 a) Look at the list of possible benefits of the HGP. Choose one that you think is the most important. Explain your choice.

   b) Look at the list of possible problems with the HGP. Choose one that you think is the most important. Explain your choice.

   c) In parts (a) and (b) above you have been considering 'naturalistic' questions. What other issues from branches of science have similar questions attached to them?

Extra activities

1 The variation in humans is the result of less than a 2% difference in DNA. Choose a partner and make a list of all the differences in your physical appearances.

2 Fred Sanger is the only Briton to have won two Nobel Prizes. Find out more about his life and work.

3 Plan a debate between John Sulston and Craig Venter. Each should put the case for their own project and why they think it is better than the other's.

4 Design the front page of a newspaper or magazine for February 2001, describing the results and the rivalry between the HGP and Celera.

The last dodo

« European artists had only captive dodos to paint »

In 1681, the last dodo died. 'As dead as a dodo' means something has been completely killed off and finished. What was the dodo and why did it die?

Discovery

In 1598, some Portuguese ships were exploring the Indian Ocean. They landed at an island covered with tropical forest. The island was called Mauritius. The sailors were glad of the rest as they were able to get fresh water and could find fresh food. They could collect fruit and hunt animals for meat.

One animal was very easy to catch. It was a large bird, bigger than a goose. It had silly little flaps instead of wings so it could not fly. It did have quite long legs and could run but stood still while the

« Sailors landed to find food and water. The dodo was an easy prey »

sailors crept up on it. It looked at them over its funny shaped beak and did not try to escape. Soon the bird was in the cooking pot. The bird didn't taste very good but it was better than ship's biscuits.

The sailors thought the bird was stupid because it did not run away from them. They called it a dodo from the word in their language that meant 'stupid'. Many other ships stopped at Mauritius and the

sailors caught dodos to eat. Some dodos were kept alive and taken back to Europe. In Europe, people laughed at the silly fat birds.

Meanwhile things were changing on Mauritius. People were moving in, building homes and chopping down the forest. They brought dogs and cats and pigs with them. Of course rats came too. The new animals ate the dodos' food and attacked the birds. The dodos had never had any competition before. They hadn't known a predator in all their millions of years living and breeding on the island. The poor dodos weren't stupid, just unprepared for the invasion of their home. One by one they died. By 1681, not a single dodo was left.

The lesson of the dodo

By the time the last dodo died, people in Europe were starting to take an interest in the world beyond their front doors. Rich people collected examples of the strange plants and animals found in faraway places. The total disappearance of this large bird with its strange face and useless wings made people think. If the dodo had become extinct, perhaps other creatures had also disappeared from the Earth in the past.

It is 3 billion years since life began on Earth. We now know that many plants and animals that lived in the past have disappeared. Often creatures died when great disasters happened. An asteroid hitting the Earth may have killed off the dinosaurs 65 million years ago.

The dodo was not the first creature to be driven to extinction by humans – nor was it the last. Wherever humans have lived they have killed off creatures. The largest and most dangerous animals have often been the targets. Mammoths, sabre-toothed tigers and giant kangaroos were hunted by primitive humans until they were all gone.

Today many species are disappearing because humans have changed the environment in which they live. When forests are cut down to make way for farms, many creatures lose their sources of food. When new species are introduced, they compete with the native creatures. Like the dodo, the native creatures often cannot compete and are driven to extinction. ■

What did the dodo look like?

It may seem strange to wonder what the dodo looked like. Although there are no photographs there are a lot of paintings showing a fat ridiculous-looking bird. Can the dodo really have been so stupid? Andrew Kitchener doesn't think so. He is curator of the Royal Museum of Scotland. He has studied the dodo and thinks that the pictures are wrong.

The paintings were done in the 17th century in Europe. The dodos had been brought all the way to Europe from Mauritius. They had been kept in cages and given a fattening diet of ship's biscuits infested with weevils. It is not surprising that the birds became fat and lazy. Kitchener has found pictures drawn by the first explorers of Mauritius that show much thinner and more athletic dodos.

Andrew Kitchener has tried to find out the truth by examining the remains of dodos. Unfortunately there are only a few bits left – a head in Oxford and a foot in London, but bones have been found in Mauritius. From these remains, Kitchener has worked out that the dodo was actually a lot slimmer than the pictures suggest and that it could run quite fast if it felt it needed to. Of course the dodo never realised it had to run away from people.

REFERENCES

Kitchener, A. (1993) Justice at last for the dodo, *New Scientist*, **139**, no. 1888, Aug.

« **Hunting drove mammoths to extinction** »

Questions

1 Look at the picture of the dodo. Why do you think people thought it was stupid?

2 Why does Andrew Kitchener think that the normal view of dodos as slow, fat and stupid birds is wrong?

3 Why didn't the dodo run away from hunters?

4 People that settled on Mauritius didn't kill all the dodos. What happened to them?

5 In the last few hundred years many animals and plants have been taken from their normal habitats and introduced into different ones. Why is the result of this bad for the environment?

Discussion

The dodo was just one species that became extinct. There are many more species of animals and plants that have become extinct in the last few hundred years. Why should we be worried about species disappearing?

Biodiversity
who needs it?

What were you doing on the 29th December – getting over Christmas? Getting ready for a New Year party? You could have being doing your bit to save the planet because 29th December is International Biodiversity Day.

Threats to species

All around the world habitats are being destroyed. In some places the destruction is deliberate. Each year the Earth loses 1% of its forests. The trees are chopped down for industry or the forest is burned to make space for crops. Other habitats are disappearing by accident. Pollution and climate change are causing corals to die. 10% of coral reefs are now lifeless piles of crumbling coral and another 30% are in danger of destruction in the next few years.

Loss of habitat means that species become extinct. One estimate suggests that in the last ten years, one-third of all species have disappeared. Most of those creatures we probably never knew

What is biodiversity?

One and three quarter million species of animals, plants, fungi and microbes have been discovered and named but it is estimated that there are probably over ten million species on the Earth. That is a lot of different organisms. Biodiversity is the number of different species that live in a habitat. A rich habitat like a tropical rain forest can be home to over 100 000 different species of flowering plant. A field of wheat that has been thoroughly sprayed with weed killer may have just the one. The tropical forest obviously has a much greater biodiversity.

« How many species of plants and animals live here? »

« ... and here? »

The Ecotron experiment

How important is biodiversity? That was the question asked by Phil Heads and his team at the Centre for Population Biology at Silwood Park just outside London. To find some answers to the question Heads and John Lawton designed the Ecotron. The Ecotron has sixteen separate compartments. Each compartment is two metres square and is provided with light, water sprinklers and air inlets and outlets. Large pots containing a small but complete ecosystem can be placed on the floor of each compartment. The ecosystems are made up of a variety of species of self-pollinating plants and small animals – aphids, snails and worms.

Shahid Naeem set up an experiment where the ecosystems were given different biodiversities. Some compartments had only nine species, others had 15 and the most diverse had 31. The ecosystems were repeated in a number of compartments and all the conditions were kept the same. The experiment lasted for 200 days. Naeem and his colleagues found that the most diverse ecosystems used up the most carbon dioxide and produced the greatest mass of plant tissue. In other words the plants grew best where there was the greatest variety of species.

David Tilman of the University of Minnesota carried out a similar experiment on the prairies of the mid-west of the USA. The experiment lasted 12 years. He divided up the prairie into 200 plots and gave each plot different amounts of nitrogenous fertiliser. On the plots given the most fertiliser a few species grew quickly and crowded out many species less able to take advantage of the extra nitrogen. The plots with the most fertiliser had the lowest biodiversity. The experiment began in 1987. In 1988 there was a serious drought. All the plots suffered from lack of water but Tilman found that the plots with the largest biodiversities coped better. When the rain returned those same plots recovered most quickly.

David Tilman's work and the results from the Ecotron suggest that ecosystems with a large biodiversity can cope best with changes in climate and are the most productive.

existed. Perhaps some of those species were vital to the natural balance of the Earth, and perhaps some may have been of use to us. Each of the hundred thousand or so species of flowering plants in the rain forest is thought to contain about six substances that could be drugs. Three to four hundred of these may prove useful in medicine. Curare, quinine and codeine were discovered in rain forest plants years ago and have been put to good medical uses. So far drug companies have made 47 useful drugs from natural substances. If the habitats are destroyed we may never get the chance to discover the rest.

Responding to the threat – or ignoring it?

The destruction of habitats has been known about for decades. Organisations such as the World Wide Fund for Nature (the World Wildlife Fund as it used to be known) have fought to protect species for many years. It is governments that decide how the various habitats of the world are used and if they should be protected.

In 1992, the United Nations called the first Earth Summit. The conference was held in Rio de Janeiro in Brazil. Delegates were sent to the conference from 78 countries and the leaders of 114 nations attended, including President Bush of the USA and Prime Minister John Major. The conference had two issues to discuss. The first issue was the changes to the climate that might be taking place. The second issue was biodiversity and the use and protection of the world's species of life. Despite months of preparation and days of talks little was decided at the conference. Some countries refused to consider anything that may have a bad effect on their economies and standard of living. In the end the 'Convention on Biological Diversity' was presented as being the way to tackle the problem. At a meeting of the Convention in the Bahamas two years later, 133 countries took part, but only 12 had come up with a plan to follow the decisions of the Convention.

« World leaders at the Earth Summit, June 1992 »

The Convention of Biological Diversity tries to encourage sustainable exploitation. This means that habitats can be used but must not be destroyed and should be allowed to recover with no loss of wildlife. The rules of the convention demand that countries cooperate but they are not enforced by law and have had little effect. Sometimes attempts to follow the rules have caused more problems.

For instance, in north-west USA the logging industry was destroying the habitat of the spotted owl. A decision was taken to protect the spotted owl by reducing the destruction of the forests. The effect was that the price of the wood used to make paper and furniture went up. To meet the demand more wood was imported from Brazil, Venezuela and Russia. In these places there were no restrictions on where the trees were felled. No one knows how many species have been lost by the destruction of forest habitats elsewhere in the world.

Saving species

The logo of WWF is the giant panda. For many people conservation means helping large creatures to survive the loss of their habitats – giant

pandas in China, orang-utans in Borneo, rhinos in Africa and Asia, tigers in India. There are many creatures all over the world that compete for our affections. It is often the survival of smaller, less appealing creatures that ensure that a habitat remains suitable for the larger animals. WWF struggles to conserve whole habitats not just the 'flagship' species that get publicity. The organisation targets governments, communities and individuals to get the message across. They are also involved in active projects to protect areas and all the species that live in them.

REFERENCES

Chefas, J. (1994) How many species do we need?, *New Scientist*, **143**, no. 1937, Aug.

« WWF (formerly the World Wildlife Fund) – a leading campaigner for the environment »

Questions

1 Give an example of an animal or plant that has been driven to extinction by human activities?

2 Why is a drop in biodiversity likely to have a bad result for us as well as the creatures that become extinct?

3 The threat to biodiversity has been known about for many years and the Earth Summit was just the biggest of the international meetings to discuss it. Why does little seem to have happened?

4 In the Ecotron experiment:
   a) What was the independent variable (i.e. the factor that was varied)?
   b) What was the dependent variable (i.e. the factor that was measured)?
   c) What were the controlled variables?
   d) Why was it important that there were enough Ecotron cubicles to have the same environments in at least two?
   e) The mixture of species in each Ecotron cubicle wasn't an exact copy of a natural habitat. Does this make the results less reliable?

5 Why are 'Save the Whale' and 'Save the Tiger' well-supported campaigns but nobody seems to want to save a worm or an insect? How is WWF tackling this problem?

Discussion

Discuss what you think can be done to solve the biodiversity problem.

WEBSITES

http://www.biodiv.org

http://www.panda.org

CHOPPING TREES
the end of the rain forests

You are probably reading this from a book made of paper. You may be sitting on a chair which has a wooden frame or leaning on a table made from wood. Wood is one of the natural resources that we use and rarely wonder where it comes from.

Once upon a time most of the Earth was covered by forest. From the polar regions to the equator, people have felled the trees. Farmers have made clearings to grow crops. Now the clearing is happening much faster as other people join native farmers. Loggers take the wood away and plantation growers clear large areas to plant cash crops like bananas.

In the tropics of South America, Africa and Asia, about 7% of the forest disappears each year. That's an area the size of two football pitches every second of every day of the year.

A walk in the Amazon rain forest

It is dull and the air is wet here under the canopy of trees. We travelled for two hours up a river from the coast and now we are being led by our guide to meet some farmers deep in the rain forest. There is very little undergrowth. The leaves of the great trees block out most of the light so few plants can grow at ground level. Wet, squelchy leaf litter covers the earth. We can see many types of insect busy breaking up the plant material. Overhead we can hear the calls of macaws and monkeys and occasionally we see an anteater. Every tree looks different – it is amazing how many different varieties there are. One or two trees bear fruits or nuts. Each tree is bound to the next by vines — some as thick as a man's arm.

At last we come to a clearing. As we step out from under the trees, the heat of the Sun hits us. This is no natural clearing. For nearly half a kilometre in each direction we can see the fallen and burnt trunks of trees. Crops are growing among the ashes. We head back into the forest to find the village belonging to the farmers who have cleared this patch of forest. Their main crop is cassava, a vegetable that is poisonous until it has been pounded, washed and cooked.

The village is a small huddle of wooden huts. The people have few possessions but they have a great knowledge of their forest. Each year or two they must clear a large area of the forest to grow their crops. The soil soon loses its fertility and the farmers move on to another patch. They leave each area for at least 20 years. In that time the trees can grow again and the forest fills in the clearing.

It takes a lot of effort for the small group of farmers to bring down the trees. Why do they do it we ask? Why not live on the food the forest can provide? That is a problem they tell us. The supplies of fruit and nuts and edible animals are very spread out. It would take far too long for hunters and collectors to find enough food to supply the village.

But the farmers have another problem. There are more people and they need more food. To grow enough crops they have had to reduce the time the forest has to recover. But when they chop down the trees after just ten years, the soil is poor and the crops do not grow well.

When the loggers look into the rain forest they can see the money they can make from it. Some of the trees are valuable. They are hard woods that people all over the world want for buildings and furniture. Thanks to a new road built by the government, the loggers can get their vehicles and machines into a fresh patch of forest.

First the trees that are due to be felled are marked. Then the tree fellers move in and drag the huge trees to the ground. Other trees fall too, pulled down by the vines that join the trees together. Next the tractors arrive to haul the trees away. They destroy every other plant in their path and leave a barren track. Tree after tree is loaded onto the lorries that rumble day and night along the road. The loggers move on leaving destruction behind them.

The solution

The population of the world is still growing. We need more food and we need resources for homes and furniture. Wood is an excellent material to make things out of and of course we still use lots of paper. How can we supply all the wood that is needed, give farmers land to grow food and still keep our forests? The answer is sustainable management of forests. Away from the tropics in the developed countries of Canada, Scandinavia, and Australia, forests are being replanted to provide wood for the future. Wild forests are protected. At least that is the theory.

In the tropics native peoples could be encouraged to use farming methods that leave most of the trees standing. Logging companies could take more care to remove only a few trees from each area and to avoid damaging the rest. Plantation owners could use crop rotation to make sure that nutrients aren't sucked out of the soil.

All these ideas mean that people must take more care of their forests. The rest of us living in cities and towns must make sure that our lifestyle does not encourage the businesses that are only concerned with making money. ∎

REFERENCE

Walker, G. (1996) Slash and grow, *New Scientist*, **151**, no. 2048, 21st Sept.

What do forests do for us?

Trees do a lot for us, even if they are left just where they are.

- The roots hold onto the soil and stop it being washed or blown away.
- The trees hold onto water. Where forests have been cleared there have been flash floods.

« Where trees have been removed floods are more likely to occur »

- Forests control the weather. Water vapour evaporates from their leaves cooling the air. In tropical areas where forests have been cleared the climate has got hotter and drier.
- A lot of the oxygen we breathe comes from forests. Trees take in carbon dioxide and convert it into wood. Burning forests releases the carbon dioxide into the air and increases global warming.
- Tropical forests have more biodiversity than cleared areas. This means that there are more species of living things in forests. Many of these creatures could be useful to us.
- Forests are a source of food. Although fruit and nut bearing trees are spread out they could be harvested.

Questions

1 What is meant by 'sustainable management of forests'? How can we use forests and keep them?

2 Look around your home. What do you have that
   a) is made of wood?
   b) is a crop grown in a tropical country, e.g. Brazil, Indonesia, Malaysia?

Extra activities

1 Draw a concept map with 'deforestation' at the centre. Make links to the answers to the following questions
   - What are the causes of deforestation?
   - What are the effects of deforestation?
   - Who benefits from deforestation?
   - Who is harmed by deforestation?

The start of the concept map is shown below:

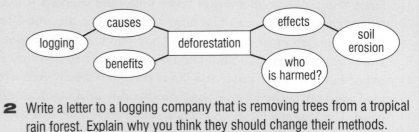

2 Write a letter to a logging company that is removing trees from a tropical rain forest. Explain why you think they should change their methods.

PESTICIDES
benefit or disaster?

Famine and sickness

The year is 1948. The place is almost any tropical country. A child is crying because it is hungry. The crops have failed again. Insect pests have attacked the plants and there is little grain left to harvest. Another child lies shivering in the heat. She suffers from malaria. Malaria is common because of the mosquitoes that infest a stagnant pool outside the village.

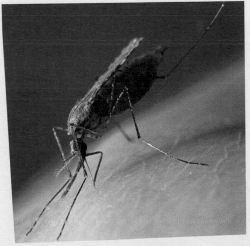

« The malaria microbe is carried by mosquitoes »

The DDT revolution

The year is 1960. The place is almost any tropical country. Children play in the dusty street through the village. They are well fed. The farmers have been able to harvest plenty of food since their land was sprayed with DDT. No one suffers from malaria since all the mosquitoes were killed. A child finds a dead bird by the side of the road. She realises that there are no birds in the sky. No birdsong fills the air like it used to do.

« No pests on this crop! »

PAUL MULLER – THE DDT MAN

Paul Hermann Muller was born in Switzerland in 1899. His father worked on the railway. Paul left school at the age of 17. He found work as a laboratory assistant in a chemical factory. He carried on studying. Three years later he was able to enter Basle University to study chemistry. In 1925, he started work for the Geigy chemical company. His first task was to investigate vegetable dyes and the substances used to tan leather. A short while later he married and had three children.

« Paul Hermann Muller, discoverer of DDT »

In 1935, Paul began some new research. He started to look for artificial pesticides. He found that a substance called DDT had been discovered in 1873. Paul spent four years working out how to make DDT. Then he tested it on lots of different pests. He found that it was a very good pesticide. His company started to make DDT in large amounts. Paul became famous as the man who invented DDT. He was awarded a Nobel Prize in 1948 and died in 1965.

DDT – a success story

DDT was put on sale in 1942. Very quickly farmers saw their crops improve. DDT killed a lot of different insect pests. It stayed in the soil for a long time so farmers didn't have to spray often. It didn't dissolve in water so wasn't washed away by rain. It seemed to have no effect on humans or other mammals. Some salesmen even ate DDT to show how harmless it was.

The British and American armies used DDT sprays on their soldiers. It killed the lice that bit the men and made life very uncomfortable.

In the USA people soon became familiar with the DDT vans that travelled along streets at night. They sprayed the roads and the gardens to kill mosquitoes that carried malaria. Children even played in the sprays.

DDT was being used in huge amounts all over the world. The chemical companies were making a lot of money from selling DDT. Everyone thought it was doing a lot of good.

'Silent Spring'

In 1957, Rachel Carson received a letter from a friend. The letter told the story of how a plane had sprayed the land with DDT. Later the friend had found lots of dead birds. The letter was more evidence for Rachel. She knew that somehow birds were being killed by DDT. DDT wasn't poisonous to birds but for some reason the number of birds was falling. Some birds of prey, like the osprey and bald eagle, had almost disappeared completely.

In 1962, Rachel published her book, Silent Spring. It warned of the dangers of DDT and the effect that it was having on bird life. The companies that made DDT didn't like her book and tried to stop it

« Pesticides are sprayed on the crops regularly »

RACHEL CARSON

Rachel Carson was born in Pennsylvania, USA in 1907. As a child she loved nature and enjoyed writing. She studied biology at Pennsylvania College for Women. Then she worked at Woods Hole Marine Biology Laboratory before completing her studies. As a trained marine biologist she got a job with the US Bureau of Fisheries. Her task was to write scripts for radio programmes about sea life. She also wrote articles for newspapers.

« Rachel Carson, who warned of the dangers of DDT »

In 1936, Rachel joined the US Fish and Wildlife Service and for 15 years wrote articles about the wonders of nature. She also wrote books, which many people bought. In 1952, she gave up her job to become a full-time writer. Her books about nature won awards.

She asked her readers to look after their environment and the creatures that lived in it. She became worried about the effects of the new chemicals that farmers were using, especially DDT. In 1962, her most important book, *Silent Spring*, went on sale and people began to take notice of her warnings. Unfortunately she was already suffering from breast cancer and died in 1964.

being published. When Rachel appeared on TV and radio the companies threatened to stop sponsoring programmes. Nevertheless people listened to her and began to realise that DDT was not good for the environment.

Why does DDT harm birds?

DDT isn't toxic to birds but if they have a lot of it in their bodies it does have some effects. The birds may become infertile or produce eggshells that are thinner than usual. The eggs are crushed when the birds sit on them in the nest.

« The numbers of birds of prey such as the osprey fell because of spraying with DDT »

Why does DDT accumulate in birds and fish?

DDT doesn't break down. Plankton absorbs molecules of DDT in the sea or rivers. Small fish eat millions of plankton. The DDT is stored in fatty tissues. Larger fish eat lots of small fish. Birds such as the osprey eat the big fish. At each stage in the food chain the DDT becomes more concentrated. The birds can have 10 million times more DDT than there is in the same amount of sea water.

DDT banned

Rachel Carson's book made people think about the use of DDT. People got together to stop it being used. In 1967, a group called Environmental Defence went to court to stop DDT being used to spray Long Island in New York. They won the court case and became the first successful environmental pressure group.

In 1970, it was discovered that some mothers in the USA had DDT in their breast milk. There was more DDT in the mothers' milk than was allowed in the cow's milk sold in shops. The headlines in newspapers made everyone worried. The USA banned the use of DDT in 1972 but companies continued to make it and sell it overseas for a few years. Even then, third world countries such as Indonesia carried on making and using DDT. Some people said DDT was the only way to control malaria.

In the year 2000, 122 countries signed a treaty. The treaty banned the use of DDT and similar substances. Rachel Carson had won at last.

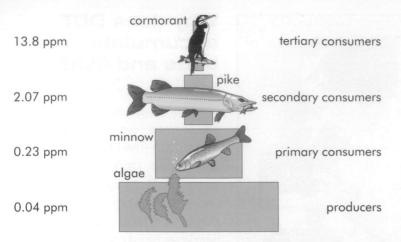

13.8 ppm	cormorant	tertiary consumers
2.07 ppm	pike	secondary consumers
0.23 ppm	minnow	primary consumers
0.04 ppm	algae	producers

« Accumulation of DDT through food chain »

« Chrysanthemum plants produce their own pesticide »

After DDT

DDT was the first artificial pesticide. Chemical companies have spent a lot of time and money making others. The new pesticides may be better for the environment for a number of reasons:

- They only kill particular pests.
- They break down into harmless substances after a short time. This means that they do not stay in the environment long enough to be carried up the food chain.

Other ways have been found to protect crops. Some chemicals stop the pests from producing offspring without actually killing them. Some crops have been genetically modified to resist pests.

Pressure groups still say that pesticides are bad for the environment. They may have unexpected effects and they take away the food supply of other animals.

Natural pesticides

Some scientists say we do not need to make artificial pesticides. Many plants produce their own chemicals that stop pests from eating them. Plants such as garlic, spearmint, rosemary and chrysanthemums all produce natural pesticides. If these plants are mixed up with crops then the crops are protected too.

Some of the plants that make their own pesticides are poisonous to humans. ■

Questions

1 Why did Paul Muller take four years to develop DDT?

2 Why was DDT sold in very large quantities very quickly?

3 Some of the disadvantages of DDT were originally seen as advantages. Explain what this means.

4 Why do you think the pesticide producers tried to stop Rachel Carson's campaign?

5 Why were large birds of prey, such as the osprey and the bald eagle, most affected by the use of DDT?

6 Since DDT was banned, malaria has returned to some places where it had been wiped out. It has been suggested that only by spraying with DDT can malaria be controlled. Do you think that DDT should be used to control malaria?

7 Some pesticides become useless after a few years. Why is this?

8 Imagine you are an organic farmer. You are not supposed to use artificial pesticides but insects are gobbling up your crop. What do you do?

Discussion

Plan a role-play debate between groups for and against the use of DDT and artificial pesticides. Characters may include:

Rachel Carson; pesticide company scientists and marketing people; environmental activists; farmers (from the developed and developing countries); doctors.

WEBSITES

http://www.nobel.se

http://www.rachelcarson.org

ACKNOWLEDGEMENTS

Science Photo Library **5l** (St.Mary's Hospital Medical School); Science Photo Library **5m**; Mary Evans Picture Library **5r**; Advertising Archive **6**; National Blood Service **9**; Wellcome Trust **11t**; Science Photo Library **11l**; American Red Cross **11r**; Alliance Pharmaceutical Corporation **13t**; Science Photo Library **13m** (Jerry Mason); Science Photo Library **22**; Rex Features London **23l**; Corbis **23r** (Bettmann); Sipa Press **23b;** Still Pictures **25** (Shehzad Noorani); Still Pictures (Mark Edwards) **26l**; Still Pictures **26r**; Science Photo Library **28t** (Geoff Tompkinson); Still Pictures **28b** (Ron Giling); Mary Evans Picture Library **29l, 29b**; Corbis **29r** (Bettman); Advertising Archive **31**; Corbis **32** (Jim Sugar Photography); Rex Features London **34, 35**; Science Photo Library **41** (Lawrence Berkeley National Laboratory); Rothamsted Laboratory **43**; Corbis **44t**; Science Photo Library **44r, 44b, 46**; Corbis **47** (Jim Zuckerman); Still Pictures **48l** (Roland Seitre), **48m**; Still Pictures **48r** (Klein)(Hubert); Rex Features London **49t**; Science Photo Library **49l**; Science Photo Library **49r** (George Bernard); Science Photo Library **51l** (A. Barrington Brown); Science Photo Library **51r**; Science Photo Library **52** (National Library of Medicine); Science Photo Library **53** (Biophoto Associates); Corbis **54l**; Rex Features London **54r**; Science Photo Library **55;** Corbis **57** (Hulton-Deutsch Collection); Oxford University **59l**; Science photo Library **59r** (K.R. Porter); Science Photo Library **61** (Will & Deni McIntyre); Science Photo Library **63** (Dr Gopal Murti); Rex Features London **65t**; Science Photo Library **65b** (Volker Steger); Science Photo Library **67** (Dr Jeremy Burgess); Still Pictures **69t** (Nigel Dickinson); Still Pictures **69b** (Edward Parker); Sipa Press **71t**; WWF **71b**; Still Pictures **72** (Jaques Jangoux); Still Pictures **74** (Nigel Dickinson); Science Photo Library **75l** (Sinclair Stammers); Still Pictures **75r** (J.P. Delobelle); Corbis **76t** (Hulton-Deutsch Collection); Still Pictures **76b** (Paul Glendell); Corbis **77** (Underwood & Underwood).

Every effort has been made to trace all the copyright holders, but if any have been overlooked the publisher will be pleased to make the necessary arrangements at the first opportunity.

INDEX

Page numbers in **bold** type show that information is contained in a picture or an illustration.